INTRODUCTION

Beware as you tear—much of this content is disturbing and potentially triggering. Every effort has been made to approach these stories with sensitivity and respect, but tales of rape, murder, torture, and violence are not appropriate for everyone. Even the most die-hard true crime fans have their limits. If you ever find yourself in need of support as you try to make sense of the dark side of humanity, please don't hesitate to reach out to the resources listed here:

National Organization for Victim Assistance referral information:
(703) 535-6682

Rape, Incest & Abuse National Network (RAINN) sexual assault hotline:
800-656-HOPE (4673)

National Suicide and Crisis Lifeline:
dial or text 988

Workman Calendars is an imprint of Workman Publishing, a division of Hachette Book Group, Inc. The Workman name and logo are registered trademarks of Hachette Book Group, Inc. PAGE-A-DAY and the PAGE-A-DAY design/logo are registered trademarks of Hachette Book Group, Inc.

The publisher is not responsible for websites (or their content) that are not owned by the publisher.

Design by Barbie Altorfer
Photo research by Sophia Reith

Cover and title page photos, clockwise from top: Vince Bucci/AFP/Getty Images, K True-Crime/Pixels, Hilda Weges/Getty Images, RGR Collection/Alamy Stock Photo

Interior photo credits are located at the end of the calendar.

Workman Calendars may be purchased in bulk for business, educational, or promotional use. For information, please contact your local bookseller or the Hachette Book Group Special Markets Department at special.markets@hbgusa.com.

ISBN 978-1-5235-3189-9

Printed in Thailand

Workman Calendars
Workman Publishing
Hachette Book Group, Inc.
1290 Avenue of the Americas
New York, NY 10104

pageaday.com

workman
CALENDARS

PHOTO CREDITS

COVER AND TITLE PAGE PHOTO INSETS (clockwise starting from top right): Vince Bucci/AFP/Getty Images, K True-Crime/Pixels, Hilda Weges/Getty Images, RGR Collection/Alamy Stock Photo.

INTERIOR: Alamy: Marcos Alvarado 1/12, CBW 11/19, Everett Collection Historical 3/25, 6/10, Everett Collection Inc 2/12, James Jackson 7/16, Johnny Jones 10/12, Susie Kearley 9/30, Keystone Press 8/13, 8/22–23, Patti McConville 10/20, Trinity Mirror/Mirrorpix 6/20–21, Serge Mouraret 9/15, Michael Neelon (misc) 7/7, NiKreative 4/16, North Wind Picture Archives 11/28–29, PA Images 8/10, Pictorial Press Ltd. 2/6, Portrait Essentials 5/8, RGR Collection 1/2, ruelleruelle 5/12, Welsh Designs/Stockimo 11/6, Xinhua 1/8, YAY Media AS 6/9, ZUMA Press, Inc. 1/29. **AP Images:** AP Photo 6/6–7, FBI/Erie Times-News via AP 1/20, David Handschuh 5/1, Joel Page 1/26, Roberto Pfeil 4/7, Steve Pfost/Newsday via AP 1/30. **Bridgeman:** Look and Learn/Peter Jackson Collection 9/10. **Courtesy Use:** Appalachian Trail Conservancy 3/26, Heritage Pest Control 2/14–15, Lansdowne Family Dental 9/4, The Canadian Press/Mark Blinch 7/9, The Historic Lizzie Borden House 11/17, True Crime Collective 12/23. **Depositphotos:** Rawpixel 7/25–26. **Getty Images:** Antagain 6/8, Bettmann 12/22, Katarzyna Bialasiewicz 9/22, boerescul 4/1, Vince Bucci 5/4, Edoardo Fornaciari 5/30–31, Brian Galbraith 2/3, Aleksandar Georgiev 1/24–25, Getty Images/Stringer 7/31, Nathan Griffith 7/18–19, guvendemir 9/23, Hailshadow 11/24, Janny2 11/30, Daniel Leal 12/5–6, Luna Marina 7/30, natasaadzic 10/5, Dana Neely 1/14, New York Daily News Archive 2/21–22, Scott Olson 4/29, Popperfoto 2/9, Alex Raths 2/23, Frederic Reglain 12/21, Screen Archives 10/3–4, shaunl/E+ 5/18, Herb Snitzer 4/11–12, Reg Speller/Fox Photos 3/17, The Ring Magazine 12/11, Underwood Archives 2/24, Hilda Weges 9/9, Westend61 12/25, Susan Wood 12/17. **Library of Congress:** Library of Congress/LC-DIG-ppmsca-28344 3/5. **Pixels:** Granger 3/12, K True-Crime 9/2. **Public Domain:** Cecilia Bleasdale 11/7–8, Capagmausuian 11/12, Dewsbury Police Station 4/2, FBI 1/14, 4/22, Manual on Uniform Traffic Control Devices 6/13–14, Murderpedia 2/16, 5/23–24, Newspaper.com 11/20. **Shutterstock:** Duncan Andison 2/17, BLGKV 8/7, Dabarti CGI 5/16–17, Nicola Devecchi 12/1, Kelvin Kho 2/26, Christophe Petit Tesson/EPA 11/10, Mark-Wu 11/13, Stephen Mulcahey 8/5, n_defender 6/5, NeagoneFo 6/1, Rix Pix Photography 8/18, solarseven 3/9, TaurusY 5/9–10, Olga Visavi 9/26–27, Westend61 8/27.

SPOTTING A KILLER

In 1963, forensic psychiatrist John Macdonald published a paper, *The Threat to Kill*. In it, Macdonald identified three behaviors he argued could be highly predictive of a future serial killer when observed in children. Known as the "Macdonald triad," they are:

- Cruelty to animals
- Repeated bed-wetting
- Setting fires

Macdonald also argued that this triad of behavior could not only predict serial murdering, but general aggressiveness.

Although Macdonald's study has been refuted multiple times, belief in its effectiveness as a tool for spotting killers remains widespread.

ON THIS DAY

Sid Vicious Trial Begins

On January 2, 1979, Sid Vicious (birth name: John Simon Ritchie) went on trial for murdering his girlfriend, Nancy Spungen. Already world famous at 21, the legendary Sex Pistols bassist, whose grubby charisma and onstage volatility had elevated the band's profile, was charged with stabbing Spungen to death the previous October in New York City's Hotel Chelsea.

In some ways, the case seemed cut-and-dried. Spungen was found with knife wounds in her stomach that seemed to match the flip knife Vicious had bought in Times Square. The "punk rock Romeo and Juliet" were addicted to heroin and had a frequently violent relationship. But others have claimed Vicious was too drugged up at the time to have committed the murder, saying a more likely scenario was a drug deal that went bad.

Either way, a jury never got the chance to decide. Vicious, who had already tried to kill himself several days after Spungen's death, fatally overdosed on February 2, 1979.

Friday, January 2 2026

Bank Holiday (SCT & NZ)

THE COUPLE THAT KILLS TOGETHER . . .

In early August 1980, lonely vocational nurse Carol Bundy had something to get off her chest. Her necrophiliac boyfriend, Douglas Clark, had been roaming Hollywood and the Sunset Strip looking for young women who might not be missed (sex workers, runaways) so he could butcher them and sever their heads. He did this often, sometimes with Bundy's assistance. Bundy unloaded the terrible secret to her ex-boyfriend, country singer John Murray.

Then Bundy panicked, thinking Murray would tell the police. After enticing Murray into his van, she killed him and cut off his head. (Although Clark likely instigated most of the couple's crimes, Bundy appeared to have been involved enough to be comfortable with the wet work.)

Bundy later confessed her crimes again. This time it was to her coworkers. Because she did not decapitate her colleagues after spilling her guts, they were able to inform the authorities. The so-called "Sunset Strip Killers" were convicted and never released. Bundy died in 2003 and Clark lived until 2023.

ANOTHER RIPPER

Part I: Just Like Old Times

In 2006, Derek Brown was in the process of turning his obsessions from fantasies into reality. A middle-aged newspaper delivery driver, Brown had been extremely interested in serial killers of the past. This macabre interest led to a desire to become one of the men he studied so intently.

Jack the Ripper, to be precise.

In honor of the famous serial killer, Brown hunted women in London's Whitechapel neighborhood. Over a period of a few weeks in 2006, Brown killed two victims—Bonnie Barrett, a 24-year-old sex worker, and Xiao Mei Guo, a 29-year-old immigrant DVD seller. Experts believe he targeted these two because he thought no one would miss them.

Fortunately, Brown was arrested before he could commit more murders. According to investigators, these two killings were intended to be just the start of a spree.

ANOTHER RIPPER

Part II: What Was Left Behind

After Derek Brown was arrested for killing two women in 2006 as part of a Jack the Ripper copycat act, police had difficulty locating any physical evidence against him. Even after an 800-hour search that included a trawl of the Thames River, the bodies of Bonnie Barrett and Xiao Mei Guo were never found.

The evidence police *did* have was in Brown's London flat. They believed that he brought the bodies of both women back there, cut them up, and disposed of the remains. The proof came in two parts: First was a handmade kit that included many items that would be of interest to a killer, such as a bow saw and waterproof sheeting. Second was the women's DNA, which police found all over the flat.

At the conclusion of his 2008 trial, the jury delivered a guilty verdict in less than three hours, not buying his claim that intruders had killed the women. Brown was sentenced to life, with a minimum of 30 years imprisonment.

ANOTHER RIPPER

Part III: Elusive Fame

"You will hear of me," Derek Brown told a friend at one point before he was arrested. "I am going to be famous."

It became clear that Brown had studied how to become a well-known killer. During the police search of his flat, they found a book Brown had checked out from the library: *Killers—The Most Barbaric Murderers of Our Time*.

Part of Brown's prediction turned out to be true: People certainly did hear of him during coverage of his trial. But famous? Not exactly.

ON THIS DAY

El Chapo Captured

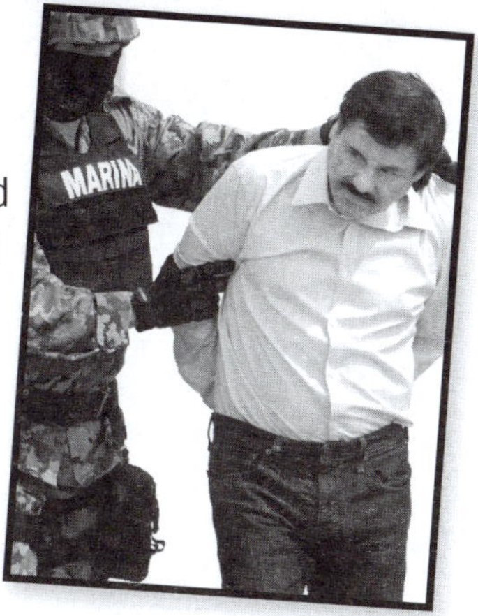

The night of January 8, 2016, Mexican marines stormed a house in the city of Los Mochis, which they believed belonged to the top sicario (assassin) in Joaquin "El Chapo" Guzmán's Sinaloa cartel. A thunderous gunfight broke out between the heavily armed groups, leaving five cartel gunmen dead. In the middle of the chaos, the marines realized Guzmán—a frequent escapee who had most recently broken out of prison the previous July—was at the house as well.

Guzmán and one of his men snuck out through a sewer. They stole a car but were ultimately arrested. Guzmán's attempts to bribe the officers failed, as did his threat to have them killed.

If not for his capture, there is little question Guzmán would have carried out that threat. While building the Sinaloa cartel through the 1990s into one of the world's biggest criminal organizations, Guzmán used staggeringly violent means to consolidate power. He once told officers that he had a hand in the deaths of more than 2,000 people, but when federal authorities charged Guzmán with 33 murders in 2018, they acknowledged that number likely fell far short of the actual toll.

"Murder often doesn't unsettle a man. In Baltimore, it usually doesn't even ruin his day."

—David Simon, crime journalist and author of *Homicide: A Year on the Killing Streets*

Friday, January 9 2026

CRIME STATS

True Crime Podcast Fans

(According to a 2023 Pew Research Center study of US podcast listeners)

- Women (44 percent) are almost twice as likely as men (23 percent) to listen to true crime podcasts.
- True crime podcast fans are almost evenly divided between Republicans and Democrats.
- The most commonly given reason for listening to true crime podcasts was entertainment (87 percent), followed by having something on while doing another activity (84 percent).
- True crime podcasts (34 percent of podcast listeners) are more popular than sports (22 percent) but less so than comedy (47 percent).

Saturday, January 10 2026

Sunday, January 11 2026

TERMINOLOGY

Cast-off pattern

This is the pattern of bloodstains that occurs when an object in motion (the weapon) leaves blood drops on surfaces. This can help forensic analysts determine everything from the type of weapon used to how many times it struck a victim.

Monday, January 12 2026

THE NURSE KILLER

Part I: Hellraising

Richard Speck had a "Born to Raise Hell" tattoo and tried hard to live up to it. Born in 1941 into a family of eight children, he suffered abuse at the hands of his stepfather and started drinking heavily while still young. Growing up near Dallas, Speck gained a reputation for boozing and starting problems. He was arrested for the first time at age 13 and dropped out of school three years later to embark on a life of petty crime.

Following many run-ins with the law, Speck was convicted in 1963 of robbery and check fraud. Once released, he went back to drifting and started to commit more serious crimes. In 1966, he robbed and raped a 65-year-old woman and may have beaten another to death.

Relocating to Chicago to stay ahead of the law, Speck started looking for work as a merchant marine. By July 13, 1966, he had been without work for days. That night, after drinking at a series of bars, he forced his way into a town house occupied by eight student nurses from South Chicago Community Hospital.

THE NURSE KILLER

Part II: The Murders and the Escape

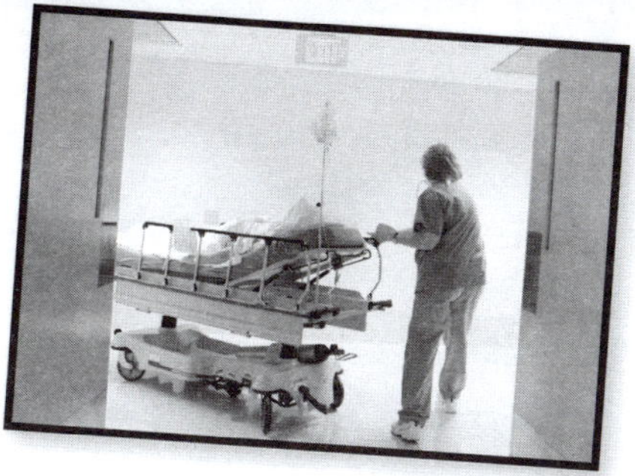

When Richard Speck broke into the town house at 2319 E. 100th Street on Chicago's far South Side, it was getting close to midnight. Likely under the influence of alcohol and prescription pills, he used a knife and handgun to threaten the six nurses he found there and bound their hands and feet with ripped-up bedsheets. When the three other nurse roommates returned home, he did the same to them.

Speck tried to convince the terrified women he was only there for money. But while he did rob them, over the course of several hours, Speck took eight of the women into another room and murdered them one by one, some by stabbing and others by strangulation. Speck also sexually assaulted one of his victims.

One nurse, Corazon Amurao, escaped her friends' fate by hiding under one of the beds. She waited until it had been quiet for hours and then screamed for help.

Just two days later, Speck attempted to kill himself and ended up in the local hospital. There, an ER doctor recognized his distinct forearm tattoo, which Amurao had described to the police.

Wednesday, January 14 2026

THE NURSE KILLER

Part III: The Trial

Richard Speck was arrested on July 17, 1966. A six-physician panel studied Speck and determined that he was a sociopath but still mentally competent to be put on trial. Court proceedings began the following April.

With the surviving nurse, Corazon Amurao, there to deliver eyewitness testimony, the jury needed less than an hour for deliberation. Speck was found guilty and sentenced to the electric chair.

Speck was never executed. An appeal dragged out for several years. Then, in June 1972, the US Supreme Court declared the death penalty unconstitutional. A few months later, Speck was resentenced to eight consecutive prison terms (one for each victim) totaling up to 1,200 years. He died from a heart attack in 1991 while still imprisoned, less than a year after the seventh and last time his parole was denied.

CRIME DATA

Men and Women

Around the world, men commit crimes at a dramatically higher rate than women. Some possible causes for this gender gap:

- Men are socialized to be more aggressive.
- Men are less likely to seek out help for mental health issues.
- Men have a greater likelihood of substance abuse, which may impair judgment.
- Men have higher levels of testosterone, which may cause heightened aggression.

TRUE CRIME QUIZ

In what year did the US murder rate grow fastest?

A. 2020

B. 1991

C. 2001

D. 1970

Saturday, January 17 2026

Sunday, January 18 2026

Answer: A. The roughly 30 percent increase in the US murder rate from 2019 to 2020 was the largest recorded since 1905.

"We make sense of violent events by choosing to deny that they happened—or by blaming the victim. This is true even if the victim is yourself."

—Sarah Kasbeer, essayist

THE COLLAR BOMBER

Part I: The Heist

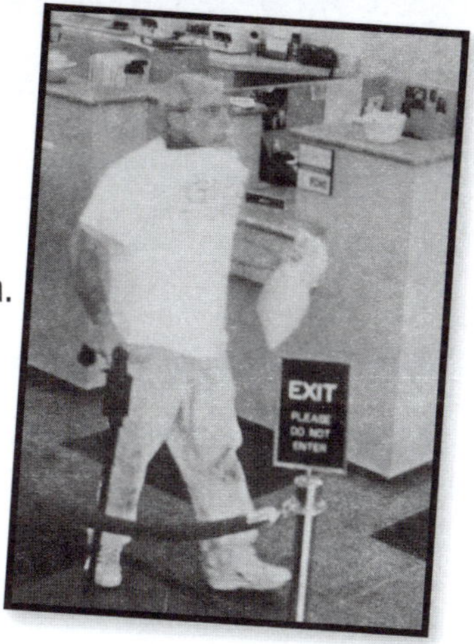

On August 28, 2003, 46-year-old pizza delivery man Brian Wells walked into a PNC Bank in Erie, Pennsylvania. He was walking with a cane and seemed to have something bulky under his T-shirt. Wells walked up to the teller window and passed the teller a note demanding $250,000. Wells said he had a bomb strapped to him and that if he didn't receive the money, the bomb would explode.

Roughly 12 minutes later, Wells walked out of the bank and drove away. But he was not a quarter-millionaire. Wells left with only $8,702.

State troopers soon caught Wells. He began to panic, telling the troopers that the bomb hanging from the metal collar around his neck was going to explode. Soon. "I don't have a lot of time," he told them.

He was right. Troopers kept a safe distance from a handcuffed Wells as they waited for the bomb squad to arrive, but the bomb exploded before it could be disarmed, killing Wells as he pleaded for help.

THE COLLAR BOMBER

Part II: The Search

After the bomb fastened to Brian Wells killed him, police started looking for culprits. Wells had said the robbery was not his idea. He claimed to have been taken prisoner by a group of men who fastened the bomb to him and gave him his orders.

Police never found the bomb-making hostage-takers. But on searching Wells's car, they did discover pages of complex instructions describing how somebody (presumably Wells) could disarm the bomb by following a series of scavenger hunt–like clues.

An investigation commenced. Based on the language in the scavenger hunt instructions, authorities believed there were multiple conspirators. Their theory was that Wells had indeed been the innocent victim in a plot that could have come straight from an action movie.

Four years after the robbery, two suspects were indicted for the plot. But their scheme turned out to be from a different kind of movie altogether.

Wells had not been an unwitting hostage: From the start, Wells had been in on the very plan that killed him.

THE COLLAR BOMBER

Part III: The Masterminds

According to authorities, the 2003 collar bomb robbery was motivated by a murder plot. Impatient to receive an inheritance, local woman Marjorie Diehl-Armstrong decided to hire a hitman to kill her father, and rob a bank to cover the fee.

Diehl-Armstrong planned the heist with friend Kenneth Barnes and ex-boyfriend William Rothstein, who helped build the bomb. (Rothstein was very helpful; he had apparently helped kill Diehl-Armstrong's former boyfriend, James Roden, and hid the corpse in his freezer after Roden threatened to expose the collar bomb plot to the police.)

The conspirators told Brian Wells the bomb was fake and that after he followed the scavenger hunt clues they had left him, he could remove it and receive a cut of the money.

Rothstein, described as the scheme's "mastermind," died from cancer in 2004. Diehl-Armstrong and Barnes were indicted in 2007 and convicted for conspiracy and armed bank robbery. Though not convicted of helping to kill Wells, Diehl-Armstrong (who may have committed other murders) was serving a sentence for Roden's murder when she died in prison in 2017.

Thursday, January 22 2026

CRIME STATS
Who Shot Ya?

There are a lot of different kinds of firearms out there. Murderers like to use pretty much all of them. However, there appear to be strong preferences. According to the FBI, in 2020, nearly 60 percent of all US gun murders and nonnegligent manslaughters involved handguns. Rifles were used in only 3 percent of similar killings, and shotguns a mere 1 percent.

CRACKED

Sanna Riitta Liisa Sillanpää

On February 21, 1999, 30-year-old Finnish IT worker Sanna Riitta Liisa Sillanpää went to an indoor shooting club in Helsinki and rented a 9mm pistol. She then opened fire at people instead of targets, killing three men and seriously injuring another.

Sillanpää fled the club, got on a bus, and rode it to the airport. At some point, she dropped the pistol in a trash can. Police detained her as she attempted to board a flight to London. Though she was found guilty of manslaughter, her sentence was waived in favor of placement in a mental hospital.

At no point during the killing, her flight, her arrest, or her trial did Sillanpää say anything about why she shot three strangers to death. The mysterious phrase she uttered after the shooting—"This is what they taught us at the FBI academy, isn't it?"—didn't provide much to go on.

Saturday, January 24 2026

Sunday, January 25 2026

THE CHURCH POISONER

On April 27, 2003, worshippers at the Gustaf Adolph Lutheran Church in New Sweden, Maine, were having coffee and sweets after Sunday service. A number of the congregants started feeling faint. Several were rushed to the hospital, where they were initially diagnosed with food poisoning. Some ended up in critical condition, including 78-year-old Walter Reid Morrill, who later died. Suspecting the coffee had been laced with arsenic, Maine CDC authorized the use of antidotes before the tests came back positive, likely saving many lives.

Questions swirled: Who in the small, tight-knit community would have done this? Then on May 2, church member Daniel Bondeson died by suicide. In the note he left, he wrote, "I acted alone. . . . I had no intent to hurt this way. Just to upset stomach, like the church goers did me."

In the investigation, authorities suspected that his motive was based in lingering anger over a dispute about different types of worship at his church after two churches in the town were consolidated into one.

Part I: The First Discovery

By 2010, Mari Gilbert had had enough trouble for several lifetimes. The Pennsylvania native had a history of abusive relationships, and her children had spent a stretch of years in foster care. Two of Mari's daughters, Sarra and Sherre, were back living with her. But her other daughter, Shannan, a 24-year-old with bipolar disorder, was on her own in Jersey City, New Jersey, making a living as a sex worker.

Late at night on May 1, Shannan was dropped off by a driver to meet a client in Gilgo Beach, a gated seaside village on Long Island. Early the next morning, she was seen running through the village screaming for help. Shannan called 911, and although she told the dispatcher, "There's someone after me," it took police roughly an hour to arrive. She was never seen again.

Shannan's family filed a missing persons report, but it took weeks for the police to link that report with Shannan's 911 call. Incensed, Mari led a media pressure campaign that finally forced police to investigate her daughter's disappearance. That December, a police dog found a woman's buried remains at Gilgo Beach, but it was not Shannan.

Part II: More Bodies Found

The remains police discovered on Gilgo Beach in December 2010 were those of Melissa Barthelemy. Soon after, police dug up three more bodies: Amber Costello, Megan Waterman, and Maureen Brainard-Barnes. The dead women fit a pattern that matched Shannan Gilbert: sex workers in their 20s who connected with clients through Craigslist.

Frustration mounted with both locals and victims' families. They felt police were playing down the fact that a serial killer was on the loose because the victims were sex workers. Suffolk Country Police Commissioner Richard Dormer told the press, "I don't want anybody to think that we have a Jack the Ripper running around Suffolk County with blood drippin' from a knife."

Contrary to Dormer's words, more bodies were dug up, including those of Shannan Gilbert, in 2011. Eleven bodies were eventually connected to the mysterious "Gilgo Beach serial killer." Local police came under fire for their conduct, and police chief James Burke, who had resisted FBI assistance in the investigation, had seemed to let the case go cold.

That changed in 2023.

LOST GIRLS

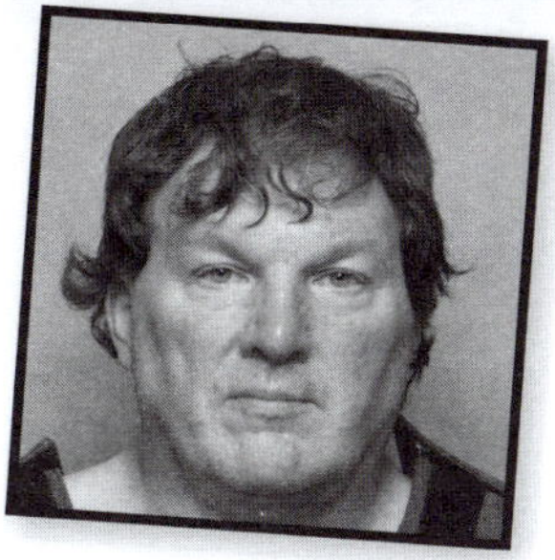

Part III: The Arrest

The Gilgo Beach serial killer case, which originally gained attention with Shannan Gilbert's panicked 911 call in May 2010, returned to the spotlight in July 2023. Rex Heuermann, a 59-year-old architect from Massapequa, Long Island, was arrested and charged with murdering four of the sex workers whose remains had been found at Gilgo Beach: Melissa Barthelemy, Maureen Brainard-Barnes, Amber Costello, and Megan Waterman. All of the "Gilgo four" women had been wrapped in a kind of camouflage burlap used by hunters.

Part of the evidence prosecutors presented against Heuermann was DNA they said connected him to the remains of the victims. Those matches were extracted from genetic samples from pizza crusts Heuermann had left in the trash outside his Manhattan office.

The arrest was reportedly made after investigators reopened an old tip about a pickup truck spotted near the last place Costello was seen alive. License plate records linked to a cell phone that had made taunting calls to one of the victim's relatives helped the investigation zero in on Heuermann.

Thursday, January 29 2026

Part IV: Wasted Opportunities

A veteran Long Island cop with swagger and a big reputation, James Burke was Suffolk County Police Department chief from 2012 to 2015. That meant he was in charge of the investigations (or what seemed at times a lack thereof) into the Gilgo Beach killings. By 2015, there were serious concerns he had negatively impacted the search for the Gilgo Beach killer.

Over the course of Burke's decades-long career, he was accused of having a relationship with a sex worker, losing his service weapon on multiple occasions, having other officers spy on his girlfriend, and physically attacking Christopher Loeb, a thief who had stolen a bag filled with sex toys and pornography from Burke's department vehicle.

In 2016, Burke was found guilty of assault and obstruction of justice and sentenced to 46 months in prison. Loeb, imprisoned for a separate crime, was present for Burke's sentencing. "Now look at us both; we're both incarcerated," he said.

Part V: Coda

Unsurprisingly, Shannan Gilbert's younger sister, Sarra, took her death and status as potential victim of the Gilgo Beach serial killer very hard. But even before Shannan's disappearance, Sarra's life had not been easy. Her early years were marked by bad relationships, not finishing high school, time in a shelter for victims of domestic violence, and mental health issues.

After Shannan's remains were found in 2011, Sarra began to spiral. In 2013, she had delusions that Shannan was still alive and the people around her were demons. Hospitalized and diagnosed with paranoid schizophrenia, Sarra stabilized. But in 2016, she stopped taking her antipsychotic medications. She was in and out of mental hospitals, and eventually lost custody of her son.

On July 23, 2016, Sarra said she was hearing voices and asked her mother, Mari, to come over. She then stabbed Mari to death with a 15-inch knife and smashed her head with a fire extinguisher. A jury did not believe Sarra's defense of insanity and found her guilty of second-degree murder. She was sentenced to 25 years in prison.

Saturday, January 31 2026

Sunday, February 1 2026

Black History Month begins (US)

TERMINOLOGY

Serienmörder

Roughly translated from German as "series-murderer," this was the term used by Berlin Criminal Police Director Ernst Gennat to describe a serial killer such as Peter Kürten, who terrorized Düsseldorf in the 1910s and 1920s.

Monday, February 2 2026

THE MORMON MANSON

Part I: The Split(s)

By 1890, members of the Church of Jesus Christ of Latter-day Saints (LDS), more commonly known as Mormons, had had enough. Formed 60 years earlier in upstate New York, the quasi-Christian LDS had been forced farther west due to the public's dislike of the Mormon practice of polygamy. But even after settling in then-remote Utah, the LDS church fought constantly with the US government. In an attempt to gain legitimacy, the LDS church officially forbade polygamy. Although some Mormon men went on living as secret polygamists, others saw the change as heretical. This split led Mormons who believed that polygamy was important to resettle in northern Mexico.

Ervil LeBaron was born into one such Mormon colony in Mexico in 1925. His brother, Joel, started the Church of the First Born of the Fullness of Time in 1955. Ervil, a hulking and violent-tempered type, had his own objectives; he began preaching ideas that went against Joel's and even tried to steal other men's wives. Eventually, Ervil was excommunicated by Joel from his church, so Ervil decided to form his own sect. Once set up as leader of the Church of the Lamb of God, Ervil did what any good schismatic leader would do: He started plotting murder.

Tuesday, February 3 2026

THE MORMON MANSON

Part II: The Feud(s)

Ervil the "Mormon Manson" LeBaron was not your average religious leader. He had 13 wives and dozens of offspring, supported himself by exploiting children of church members for slave labor in appliance repair shops, and spent more time plotting murder than preaching.

Ervil decided any religious leaders who didn't accept that he was God's sole earthly prophet needed to die. First to go was Ervil's brother, Joel, shot to death in 1972 by one of Ervil's henchmen. Ervil served a year in prison for that but got out on a technicality. In 1974, two members of the late Joel's faction were killed in a coordinated firebomb assault intended to kill another of Ervil's brothers.

In the following years, Ervil and his followers perpetrated at least 20 assassinations. Among their alleged victims were former supporters and family members. The 1977 shooting death of rival polygamist leader Rulon Allred (according to one of his wives and a stepdaughter) finally led to Ervil's imprisonment. He died in a Utah state prison in 1981, possibly from suicide, following a bout of depression.

THE MORMON MANSON

Part III: The Aftermath

Despite the death of Ervil LeBaron, his nomadic and semi-feral Church of the Lamb of God kept on with his work. That is, they continued practicing polygamy, living hand to mouth across Mexico and the United States, and committing murder.

Before dying in prison in 1981, Ervil had created a hit list of his imagined enemies. Many of those people were ultimately gunned down, including four victims killed in the so-called "4 O'Clock murders," which all happened at 4:00 p.m. on June 27, 1988, in three different Texas locations. Ervil's followers' crime spree continued for years. They racked up more murders, kept squabbling with other Mormon sects, and took on hobbies, like gun running, that had little to do with their die-hard belief in having multiple wives.

In 2019, nine Mormons connected to the extended LeBaron clan were shot dead. This apparently had nothing to do with Ervil's reign of posthumous terror. Instead, it was the tragic result of a long-running conflict with drug cartels over farms the LeBarons had operated for generations.

THE GREAT FORTUNE TELLER RAID

April 20, 1934, was the culmination of an extensive New York police investigation into one of the most "dangerous" trends sweeping the city: fortune tellers.

The "Statute of Prediction" made it a crime to be paid for telling people's fortunes. Normally this was not seen as a high-profile issue. But starting in the late 1920s, "tea rooms" proliferated where guests could ostensibly pay for lunch or a coffee while fortune tellers told them what lay in their futures.

The tea rooms' popularity with women—especially working-class women—caused something of a moral panic in the city. Disgruntled husbands and newspapers accused fortune tellers of inciting "a wave of melancholia" among women due to their sometimes frightening predictions. This led to an extensive sting investigation led by New York's top female officer, Mary Shanley, who thought fortune telling was an evil that needed to be eradicated.

The 1934 raid targeted three tea rooms and netted about a dozen fortune tellers. Although undercover operations of this kind no longer happen, fortune telling remains a misdemeanor in New York.

Friday, February 6 2026

Waitangi Day (NZ)

CRIME STATS

Personal Weapons

The FBI has statistics for many things. More than you can imagine. For instance: The agency calculated that in 2019, roughly 4 percent of all homicides in the United States were committed by what they called "personal weapons." What is a personal weapon? The FBI describes it as "hands, fists, feet, etc." Which begs the question: What's an "etc." personal weapon?

Saturday, February 7 2026

Sunday, February 8 2026

TRUE CRIME QUIZ

Which of the following people was *not* part of the group that killed Abigail Folger, Wojciech Frykowski, Steven Parent, Jay Sebring, and Sharon Tate in 1969's "Helter Skelter" murders?

A. Charles "Tex" Watson

B. Linda Kasabian

C. Charles Manson

D. Susan Atkins

Monday, February 9 2026

Answer: C. Manson ordered the killing but stayed away from the deed itself.

GUILT BY GOOGLE

James Craig of Aurora, Colorado, was charged in 2023 with murdering his wife, Angela Craig. Authorities claimed that James had bought arsenic and cyanide, which he then mixed into Angela's protein shakes. They also charged that he had made suspicious Google and YouTube searches, including:

- "How many grams of pure arsenic will kill a human"
- "Is arsenic detectable in autopsy"
- "Top 5 undetectable poisons that show no signs of foul play"
- "How to make poison"

WHO DID BUGSY KILL?

Few mobsters can claim the historical impact of Benjamin "Bugsy" Siegel. A Brooklyn-raised hooligan, he supposedly received his nickname due to a wicked temper; "crazy as a bedbug" was one criminal colleague's take (true to form, Siegel *hated* the nickname and let people know it). Siegel worked as an enforcer and bootlegger for Meyer Lansky's Prohibition-era gang, later helping Lansky start up Murder Inc., one of the American underworld's most efficient and feared assassination cartels.

Siegel gained power, wealth, and infamy during the 1920s and 1930s, establishing a reputation as a dashing and flashily dressed but remorseless gangster. He also took part in his share of murders, killing as many as 30 people. Among his most famous hits was the 1931 assassination of Giuseppe "Joe the Boss" Masseria. That hit, engineered by Lucky Luciano, ended a chaotic New York gang war and led to the establishment of the "Five Families" Mafia syndicate.

WHO KILLED BUGSY?

At some point, the East Coast got too hot for Bugsy Siegel. He was sent out west in the late 1930s to help make the region friendly for organized crime. Siegel not only built out and professionalized bookmaking and the drug trade through Mexico, he brought a glitzy sheen to Los Angeles organized crime. In addition to running glamorous offshore casinos, Siegel socialized with the likes of Frank Sinatra and Jean Harlow.

In the 1940s, Siegel pioneered a new criminal frontier by spearheading the reinvention of flyspeck desert town Las Vegas into a gambling mecca. He took over development of the Flamingo, an audacious new casino that took advantage of Nevada's legalized gambling and aimed to draw customers through unprecedented (in America, at least) luxury. Though the Flamingo eventually became a draw, discontent over cost overruns and a delayed opening combined with a long list of enemies put a target on Siegel's back.

On June 20, 1947, about six months after the Flamingo's grand opening, Siegel was shot dead by a sniper while sitting in his Beverly Hills mansion. His killer was never identified.

TERMINOLOGY

What kind of killing?

According to the FBI's Uniform Crime Reporting program, criminal homicides are broken into two primary categories:

- Murder and nonnegligent manslaughter: The "willful" (intentional) "killing of one human being by another."
- Manslaughter by negligence: "The killing of another person through gross negligence."

THE RAT GAMBIT

In 2015, Christopher Baker of Sunderland, England, went to the Borneo Buffet on Valentine's Day (yes, alone) and was shocked to discover a rat in the restaurant. He believed this entitled him to a free £7.25 (about US $9) buffet. The problem for Baker's plan was that CCTV showed him taking the rat out of his pocket. "People like him deserve the death penalty," declared the Borneo Buffet's frustrated owner. This punishment was not delivered, but Baker was instead fined £60 (about US $76), plus the cost of the meal.

Saturday, February 14 2026 Valentine's Day

Sunday, February 15 2026

THE WOLF'S GIRL

By the time James Marlow was released from Folsom California State Prison in May 1986, the so-called "Folsom Wolf" had been married six times and spent much of his life committing robberies and home invasions, doing speed, and getting neo-Nazi tattoos. He already had his soon-to-be seventh wife waiting for him on the outside. Cynthia Coffman was more drifter than career criminal but liked enough of what she saw in Marlow to marry him after knowing him for just a few weeks and having "Property of the Folsom Wolf" tattooed on her rear.

The two didn't wait long before starting their crime spree. Starting in October, Marlow and Coffman started kidnapping, robbing, and strangling women to death. They claimed four victims before being arrested in November. Both were convicted and sentenced to death, Coffman's attempted "Patty Hearst" defense (she claimed Marlow had brainwashed her) not saving her from death row.

Do crime rates really rise during a full moon?

Answer: No. A 1985 review of 37 studies of criminal behavior during different lunar phases found no correlation. Its author ascribed this belief as “a willingness to accept any departure from chance as evidence of a lunar effect.”

KUNG FU KILLER

David Carradine, an actor best known for his lengthy stint as a wandering martial arts warrior in the series *Kung Fu*, was found dead in a Bangkok hotel room in June 2009. His naked body was discovered in the room's closet with cords wrapped around his genitals and neck. Local police immediately determined, unsurprisingly, that Carradine had died while attempting some variation of autoerotic asphyxiation.

Not so fast, Carradine's family and their lawyer, Mark Geragos, declared just days later. It seemed more likely to Geragos that the secretive Carradine had in fact been murdered to stop him from his mission to uncovering an underground martial arts gang. Sadly, this secret has never been revealed.

THE NERDY MURDERER

Part I: The Loner

There wasn't much that Joel Rifkin could do to belong as a young man. Born in 1959 and raised mostly on Long Island by his adopted parents, Rifkin was intelligent (his tested IQ was 128) but suffered from undiagnosed dyslexia and couldn't pull it together academically. Though his parents were described as thoughtful and caring people, Rifkin was an awkward, slouchy, and insecure boy who never quite fit in. He was incessantly teased in school by bullies who gave him nicknames like the "Turtle" and pulled pranks on him. Constantly bullied and ostracized, Rifkin seemed to develop a need for power and control, a trait commonly seen in people who become killers. He also developed two habits that would lead to tragic consequences: marinating in violent sex fantasies and hiring sex workers.

After high school, a string of disappointing jobs and unfinished stints at community college left Rifkin drifting. In 1987, the same year his father died by suicide after a long struggle with cancer, Rifkin was arrested for soliciting a sex worker who turned out to be an undercover police officer.

Then, in 1989, around the time his lonely and aimless life really began to come apart, Rifkin started killing.

THE NERDY MURDERER

Part II: The Killer

Joel Rifkin had been collecting books and news stories on serial killers for years before he started acting on what he learned from them. Operating out of his mother's house on Long Island and apparently inspired by Alfred Hitchcock's grisly 1972 serial killer movie *Frenzy*, he would troll New York for sex workers, who became his victims.

The first murder that Rifkin later confessed to happened in 1989. The severed head of Heidi Balch, a sex worker Rifkin had picked up and murdered in his mother's house, was found on a New Jersey golf course; her legs were found in a nearby creek. The next year, he killed and dismembered another sex worker, Julie Blackbird, also in his mother's house.

Rifkin's killings moved into a different stage in 1991. That year, he bought four 55-gallon steel drums, and in just a few months used them to dispose of four new victims. Over the next two years, he strangled multiple women, chopping up their bodies and dumping their remains all across the Tri-State area.

By the time Rifkin was arrested in 1993, he had killed up to 17 women and possibly many more.

THE NERDY MURDERER

DAILY NEWS
L.I. murder suspect tells cops:
I KILLED 17 WOMEN
STORIES ON PAGES 2 & 3

Part III: The Talker

Late on the night of June 28, 1993, New York State troopers attempted to stop a pickup truck without license plates driven by Joel Rifkin. In the ensuing chase, Rifkin crashed. When the officers searched the vehicle, they discovered the rotting corpse of Tiffany Bresciani (Rifkin had killed her days earlier and left her body in his stifling hot garage). Within hours, and before he even had a lawyer, Rifkin started talking. He drew maps to show the remote locations where he had dropped the women's bodies—hoping decomposition would remove incriminating physical evidence.

The most prolific serial killer in New York history, Rifkin was dubbed the "Ripper" by the *New York Post* and tried for murder in two separate trials. One defense expert claimed that Rifkin had "adopted child syndrome," a bogus idea that adoptees are more likely to become serial killers. This, and Rifkin's insanity claim, failed to convince a jury.

Rifkin was sentenced to more than 200 years in prison.

Saturday, February 21 2026

Sunday, February 22 2026

DROPS OF DEATH

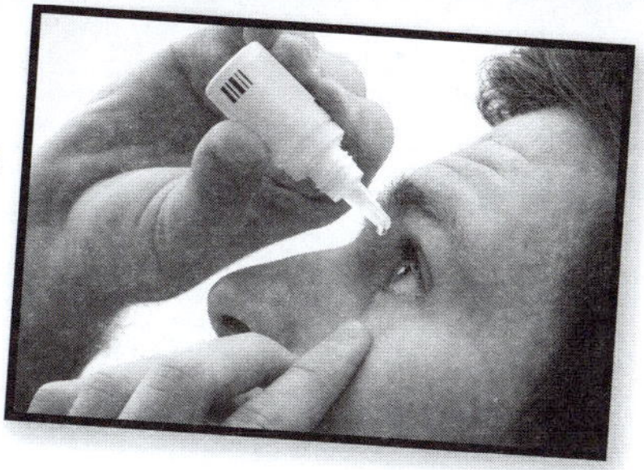

Wisconsinite Jessy Kurczewski told police in October 2018 that Lynn Hernan, a family friend who had been in her care, was unconscious. When authorities arrived at Hernan's home, they found she was dead in an apparent suicide, with crushed medication on her chest and by her side. After the medical examiner discovered lethal amounts of tetrahydrozoline (an ingredient in some eye drop brands) in Hernan's systems, suspicions were aroused.

Kurczewski was arrested in July 2019. She was charged with stealing nearly $300,000 from Hernan and then dumping six bottles of Visine into Hernan's water. While Kurczewski claimed Hernan had been suicidal and had gifted her that money (part of which she allegedly gambled away in casinos), she was found guilty of homicide and theft in 2023 and sentenced to life in prison.

CRIME TECH

The Polygraph

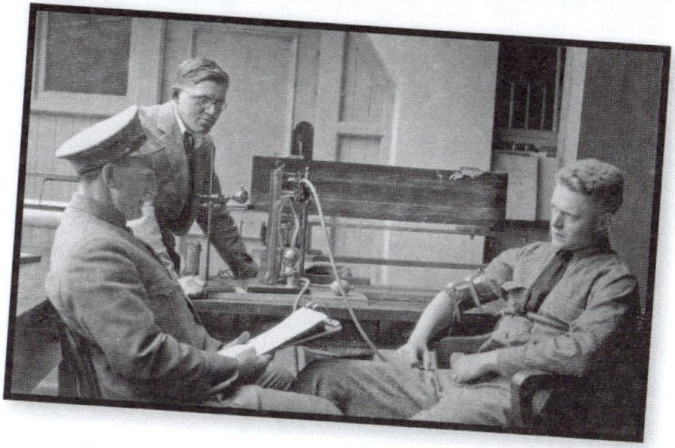

Polygraph machines, or "lie detectors," came into wide usage in the early 20th century. With some variations, the polygraphs used today are essentially the same. Hooked up to a person via straps and wires on the chest and hand, and sometimes the arm, polygraphs are believed by their proponents (including many law enforcement agencies) to determine whether the subject is being truthful about questions they are asked. While a truth-telling machine would be great, polygraphs have been repeatedly debunked: It turns out they are just measuring anxiety. As one might imagine, a police interrogation will generate anxiety in the guilty and the innocent alike.

"One of television's greatest contributions is that it brought murder back into the home where it belongs. Seeing a murder on television can be good therapy. It can help work off one's antagonism. And, if you haven't any antagonisms, the commercials will give you some."

—Alfred Hitchcock, filmmaker who created many on-screen murders

Wednesday, February 25 2026

CARTEL GATORS

During a 2008 raid on a favela in Rio de Janeiro, Brazilian police seized a pair of small alligators. They said that gangsters who kept them were feeding their enemies to the reptiles.

That was not true, claimed the father of one alleged crook. According to him, the gangsters had indeed tried to dispose of the corpse of one of their victims that way. But it turned out that the alligator was not interested in eating a human body.

THE STONEMAN MURDERS

Part I: Mumbai

Beginning in 1985, police in Mumbai, India, started noticing a pattern of sinister crimes in the city's King's Circle and Sion neighborhoods. Morning after morning, another corpse would turn up with a couple of specific characteristics. First, all of the victims were unhoused. Second, they were sleeping alone when attacked. Third, each had their heads crushed by a large stone weighing up to 60 pounds.

One man, a waiter, survived the attack, but was unable to give a description of his assailant. This left the police looking for a large man who could lift heavy stones. By the time the killings stopped in 1988, 12 victims had been claimed.

But the so-called "Stoneman" was not finished.

THE STONEMAN MURDERS

Part II: Kolkata

In June 1989, police in Kolkata, India, were confronted with a series of disturbing killings that mirrored the murders haunting the city of Mumbai. Throughout that summer, corpses of unhoused people sleeping rough on the streets were discovered in isolated areas of Kolkata, dead from head trauma caused by large stones or pieces of concrete. Was this the "Stoneman" killer striking again?

Over the course of six months, 13 victims were found. Many suspects were rounded up. But just like the Mumbai case, a lack of evidence kept police from pressing charges. The Kolkata killings stopped in 1989. But in 2002, another spate of murders occurred in a town in the state of Madhya Pradesh, when four men were murdered in the dead of night by an attacker who smashed their heads in with a stone, hammer, or spade.

An assailant was never caught, and authorities still don't know if the attacks were committed by one person, multiple killers, or copycats.

Saturday, February 28 2026

Sunday, March 1 2026

Women's History Month begins (US)

Murder categories

When it comes to breaking down the differences between different categories of murderers, the devil is in the details.

"Spree killers" are often mistaken for "serial killers." The chief difference between the two is that a spree killer kills two or more victims in a very compressed period of time. Serial killers might do that as well, but they have periods of inactivity before killing again.

Shower Posse

One of Jamaica's legendary crime bosses was Lester Lloyd Coke. As leader of one of the island's most feared gangs, the Shower Posse, he ruled over a drug smuggling empire that spread cocaine and marijuana across the United States during the 1980s. Explanations for his gang's name vary: Some say it was for all the gifts Coke showered on people in the Kingston neighborhood where he inspired deep loyalty; others for all the bullets they showered indiscriminately at their enemies. Shower Posse shoot-outs and assassinations may have claimed as many as a thousand lives.

Because of the Shower Posse's connection to Jamaica's Labour Party and the part Coke likely played in the 1976 shooting of Bob Marley, conspiracy theories have long swirled around the gang, including the belief they were supported, at one point, by the CIA. A key point of evidence for conspiracists was the suspicious manner of Coke's passing: He burned to death in a jail cell in 1992 while awaiting extradition to the US.

“MARM” MANDELBAUM

Part I: Rise to Power

In some ways, the life of Fredericka “Marm” Mandelbaum was an American success story. She landed in New York City in 1850 and scratched out a living as a street peddler. But by the time of her death, the once-poor German Jewish immigrant was one of the most famous women in America. Her fame and eventual fortune did come from a life of crime, but street peddling could only pay so much.

In the late 1850s, Mandelbaum started recruiting the poor children who roamed Manhattan’s Lower East Side as pickpockets and thieves, fencing their stolen goods. In a few years, she had adult thieves bringing her loot to sell from a storefront on Rivington Street. Her network of contacts, impeccable organization, and high standards turned her fencing operation into a cash machine. She sometimes provided funds for large-scale thefts like bank robberies in exchange for a cut of the proceeds. Goods from around the country (including loot from 1871’s Great Chicago Fire) passed through her hands.

By the 1870s, Mandelbaum was one of New York City’s most powerful crime lords and a powerful political boss, to boot. But the bigger she became, the more the police wanted to take her down.

"MARM" MANDELBAUM

Part II: Fall from (Criminal) Grace

"Marm" or "Mother" Mandelbaum claimed to be nothing more than a humble, successful, synagogue-attending Lower East Side dry goods merchant. In reality, the many political bosses and merchants wanting her attention knew that she was the premier fence for stolen merchandise on the East Coast in the 1880s. It was estimated that goods worth around $10 million (about $300 million today) passed through the hands of the woman a Brooklyn newspaper called "a most respectable and philanthropic receiver of stolen goods."

In 1884, New York City's District Attorney Peter B. Olney hired Pinkerton private detectives (too many city cops were on Mandelbaum's payroll) to infiltrate her operation. An undercover agent pulled off a sting fencing supposedly stolen silks, leading to Mandelbaum's arrest.

But when her trial began that December, there was one problem: no defendant. Having easily made bail, Mandelbaum relocated herself to Ontario, Canada. By all accounts, she was terribly bored in the Great White North. When Mandelbaum died in 1894, her body was taken to New York City for burial, but stories of her criminal genius remained so widespread that some speculated that she was still alive and that there was nothing but stones in the coffin.

"MARM" MANDELBAUM

Part III: The Protégés

"Marm" Mandelbaum's criminal success was based largely on only working with the best in the underworld. Because great thieves are not just born but made, she briefly ran a school on New York City's Lower East Side where some of the most successful crooks around taught young children the ways of crime. (After a policeman's son enrolled, Mandelbaum supposedly shut the school out of an abundance of caution.)

Mandelbaum had many criminal confederates over the years, such as George Leonidas Leslie, aka the "King of the Bank Robbers." Leslie ran the 1869 Ocean National Bank heist, then the largest robbery in New York City history, for Mandelbaum.

Mandelbaum also had a small team of female crooks, mostly pickpockets and blackmailers. Sophie Lyons, a protégé of Mandelbaum's who supposedly lifted her first pocketbook at age six, later became the country's most infamous "confidence woman." Even Harry Houdini, the premier authority on fakery, called Lyons "a consummate actress" who could bilk any man out of just about anything. She later renounced crime and went on to write an autobiography, *Why Crime Does Not Pay*.

TERMINOLOGY

Double jeopardy

This is the legal rule that states nobody can be prosecuted twice for the same crime. It derives from the Constitution's Fifth Amendment clause, which says nobody can "be subject for the same offense to be twice put in jeopardy of life or limb."

Saturday, March 7 2026

Sunday, March 8 2026

Daylight Saving Time begins (US & CAN)

CYBER CRIME

Online Bank Robbery

The internet was officially launched in 1983. The first known instance of it being used for a bank robbery took place 11 years later. A group of Russian hackers led by Vladimir Levin broke into the Citibank system. Over the summer of 1994, they transferred more than $10 million into bank accounts they had set up around the world. Authorities finally lured Levin to London in 1995, where he was arrested and, after a lengthy extradition fight, sentenced to three years in prison.

CRIME STATS

Stranger Danger

Most crime fiction involves people killed by people they do not know. But in reality, the opposite is true. Among the murders recorded in the United States in 2022 where the killer's relationship to the victim was known, 3,560 were committed by acquaintances, as compared to 1,998 committed by strangers.

THE MURDER OF VICKI MORGAN

Part I: A Bad End

On July 7, 1983, Vicki Morgan and her roommate, Marvin Pancoast, were in a bad place. The two had met a few years earlier as patients in a mental health center. By this point the two were out of work, trying to make ends meet, and would soon be forced to leave Morgan's luxury North Hollywood condo.

Well after midnight, Pancoast walked into a nearby police station and said, "I just killed someone." Officers went to the condo and found Morgan's dead body in bed, with a bloodied baseball bat nearby.

The 30-year-old Morgan had once been a model, the mistress of one of the richest men in America, and a would-be whistleblower who claimed to have evidence of salacious scandals in the Reagan White House. After her death, some believed the killing was part of a larger conspiracy.

THE MURDER OF VICKI MORGAN

Part II: The Affair

Thirteen years before her murder in 1983, Vicki Morgan was a recently married 17-year-old runaway whose life changed completely when she met Alfred Bloomingdale. Heir to his family's department store fortune, the married 53-year-old Bloomingdale paid for Morgan's divorce and set her up as his mistress.

Bloomingdale romanced Morgan in style. He lavished her with gifts, took her on overseas trips, and paid her up to $18,000 a month. She spent much of the 1970s blowing through money, having affairs with the rich and famous (including the king of Morocco), breaking up and reconnecting with Bloomingdale, and worsening various addictions. After Bloomingdale joined President Ronald Reagan's administration, Morgan circulated in the White House and later claimed to have juicy stories to tell.

In 1982, Bloomingdale's wife, Betsy, cut off Morgan's payments just months before he died of cancer. Soon after, Morgan filed a multimillion-dollar palimony suit claiming her dying lover was a sadist who loved to brutalize women.

THE MURDER OF VICKI MORGAN

Part III: Not Going Quietly

When Vicki Morgan was beaten to death in 1983, Marvin Pancoast confessed almost immediately. However, he later recanted and told a different story. At Pancoast's murder trial in 1984, his lawyer alleged that other mysterious individuals had in fact murdered Morgan to keep her from spilling secrets about the White House.

For years, Morgan had told wild stories about scandalous goings-on with Bloomingdale and other famous people, some in the Reagan White House. Pancoast's attorney claimed that the government was in possession of videotapes showing her having sex with different high-ranking people (among them Reagan confidante Edwin Meese).

The videotapes, if they ever existed, never came to light. Pancoast, who pleaded not guilty by reason of insanity, was convicted of Morgan's murder and died in prison in 1991.

CHARLES WHITMAN'S BRAIN

In 2014, a viral news story reported that the University of Texas at Austin lost 100 brains. A brief explanation: The school's Psychology Department had been collecting brains from autopsies of mental patients dating back to the 1950s and preserving them in big glass jars of formaldehyde. It was later revealed that most of those brains that had gone missing were destroyed as biological waste, but not all. Clearly, the university did not keep very good track of its brains.

Among the brains that may have been lost was that of Charles Whitman. One of America's most infamous mass shooters, Whitman was a 25-year-old ex-Marine who murdered his wife and mother in 1966 before climbing a tower at UT-Austin with a rifle and murdering 14 strangers. In his suicide note, Whitman requested an autopsy to find out the cause of his headaches. It turned out that Whitman, who was shot dead by police, had a tumor on his amygdala, which is a part of the brain that helps regulate behavior and decision-making.

Saturday, March 14 2026

Sunday, March 15 2026

Mothering Sunday (UK)

GANGLAND TALES
COVID Crimes

Some people used government assistance to save their businesses during the COVID-19 pandemic. Of course, businesses take all forms. In 2023, 30 members of the Milwaukee gang known as the “Wild 100s” were charged with stealing millions of dollars in pandemic relief money to get on with the work of crime. According to the indictment, the “Wild 100s” filed fake claims and used the funds to buy guns, drugs, and jewelry. They also allegedly paid a gunman $10,000 to assassinate a rival’s family member, only for him to kill the wrong person.

THE MYSTERY WOMAN OF HAGLEY ESTATE

In April 1943, some teenage boys were sneaking around the grounds of Hagley Hall, an 18th-century estate in Worcestershire, England, when they made a surprising discovery: the skeleton of a woman hidden in the hollow of an elm tree.

Investigators were at a loss. Aside from some ragged clothing and a fake gold wedding ring, there were no clues to the woman's identity. A scrap torn from her dress and shoved in her mouth indicated the possibility of death by suffocation.

The mystery sparked many theories, ranging from ritual killing and witchcraft to claims the woman was a murdered German spy. In 1953, a letter sent to a local paper claimed that the only person who knew the answer to the "Wych elm crime" was "now beyond the jurisdiction of the earthly courts."

Not long after the discovery, somebody wrote, "Who put Bella down the wych elm?" in chalk on a wall in nearby Birmingham. Since then, variations on that message have continued to crop up all around the city, a fittingly haunting coda to a still unsolved mystery.

"Psychologists theorized that women's appreciation of true-crime literature may arise from a fear of crime and a wish to learn how to avoid it; it was further theorized that what women learn from true-crime books just makes them grow more afraid and buy more true-crime books."

—Rafil Kroll-Zaidi, "Findings," *Harper's Magazine*

TRUE CRIME TRIVIA

Which film was *not* inspired by a real true crime story?

A. *In Cold Blood* (1967)

B. *The Bling Ring* (2013)

C. *Extremely Wicked, Shockingly Evil and Vile* (2019)

D. *Longlegs* (2024)

Answer: D. In an interview on the *Inside Total Film* podcast, *Longlegs* director Osgood Perkins said, "I can't look at real things. I don't like them. They don't sit well with me. I don't want to know. . . . All this stuff couldn't be more fictionalised and totally made up."

HIDING OUT

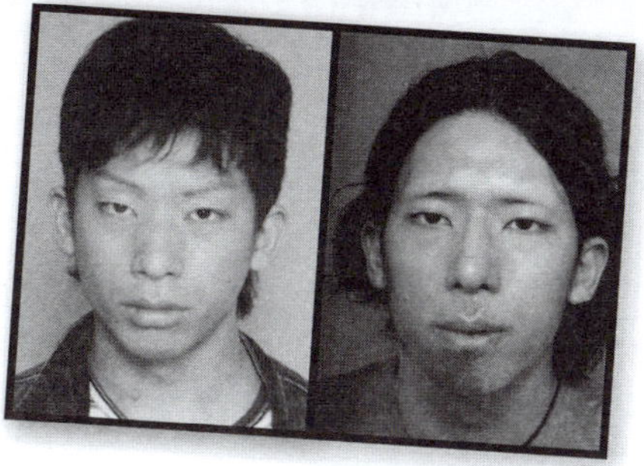

In March 2007, the body of British teacher Lindsay Ann Hawker was found at an apartment near Tokyo. One of her students, Tatsuya Ichihashi, had raped, murdered, and left her in a sand-filled bathtub on the balcony.

Over the next two years, while on the lam, Ichihashi avoided arrest by taking some extreme measures to change his appearance. These self-inflicted cosmetic procedures included:

- Tying his nose with thread and a needle to make it skinnier
- Slicing off his lower lip with scissors
- Cutting moles off his face with a box cutter

Ichihashi was finally arrested in 2009 after he went to a plastic surgery clinic for more work and staff reported him to the police.

KILLERS THESE DAYS

In his 1946 essay "Decline of the English Murder," George Orwell wrote about one of the great English pastimes: reading about murders in the newspaper. According to Orwell, the "great period" of English murder was from 1850 to 1925. Popular stories about Victorian killers such as Jack the Ripper and "The Rugeley Poisoner," Orwell said, involved powerful motives (respectability, money, secret passions), and complex investigations that satisfied the public's hunger for drama and tragedy.

Orwell's concern was that the contemporary murders he read about seemed so dull in comparison. He was disappointed by 1944's "Cleft Chin Murder," where a British teenager and an American army deserter went on a six-day crime spree that ended in the senseless murder of a cab driver. Finding the crime's background of "the anonymous life of the dance-halls and the false values of the American film" depressing, Orwell expressed nostalgia for the good old days of "domestic poisoning dramas," which he called the "product of a stable society."

Saturday, March 21 2026

Sunday, March 22 2026

TRUE CRIME QUIZ

On January 29, 1979, 16-year-old Brenda Spencer opened fire on an elementary school near her San Diego, California, home with a scoped .22 rifle, a Christmas present from her father. After firing nearly 40 shots over about 20 minutes, she hit 11 children and adults, killing 2.

When asked by a reporter, what answer did Spencer give for the killings?

A. "I always hated that school."

B. "It was better than killing myself."

C. "I really just don't know."

D. "I don't like Mondays."

Answer: D. Spencer's answer later inspired a song of the same name by the Boomtown Rats.

Part I: Frank Baumgarteker

When Prohibition started in 1920, many breweries and winemakers either went out of business or figured out how to adapt. Frank Baumgarteker was the latter. An enterprising Austrian immigrant who set up shop in Los Angeles, he had obtained one of the rare, valuable government licenses that allowed him to legally make wine, but only for purposes not involved with drinking for fun (religious ceremonies, medical purposes, etc.). Baumgarteker had become quite prosperous during Prohibition, knitting together a mix of businesses (wineries, vineyards, ranches) that made him a millionaire.

Then one day in 1929, Baumgarteker told his wife that a few "Italians from Chicago" had shown up, making an offer for his business that they thought he couldn't refuse. But refuse he did. Then on November 25, Baumgarteker disappeared while delivering the payroll to one of his companies.

MOB WINE

Part II: More Go Missing

In January 1930, just a couple of months after Frank Baumgarteker disappeared after apparently refusing the request of Chicago mobsters to sell them his various valuable wine-making businesses, his winery in Los Angeles's Lincoln Heights neighborhood was raided by federal agents. Hundreds of thousands of gallons of wine and spirits were seized. Yet, even though authorities managed to find the booze, they failed to locate Baumgarteker's body or his attackers. Within the next year, at least two of Baumgarteker's partners also went missing, as well as a Los Angeles gangster reportedly connected to the winery owner's disappearance.

Mysteries multiplied over the years. Rumors spread that Al Capone had been one of the gangsters to threaten Baumgarteker. In 1937, Baumgarteker's widow went to court to claim the life insurance money on policies he had taken out worth about $8 million today.

A man alleging to be connected to Baumgarteker's killers claimed in 1938 to know where his body was buried. But a fruitless search in a San Bernadino canyon turned up nothing. Tips suggesting Baumgarteker had absconded to Mexico also came to nothing.

Wednesday, March 25 2026

MURDER IN THE MOUNTAINS

From 1974 to 2019, there were 13 known murders on the more than 2,000-mile-long Appalachian National Scenic Trail, a popular footpath that attracts roughly 2 million hikers a year. Among them were:

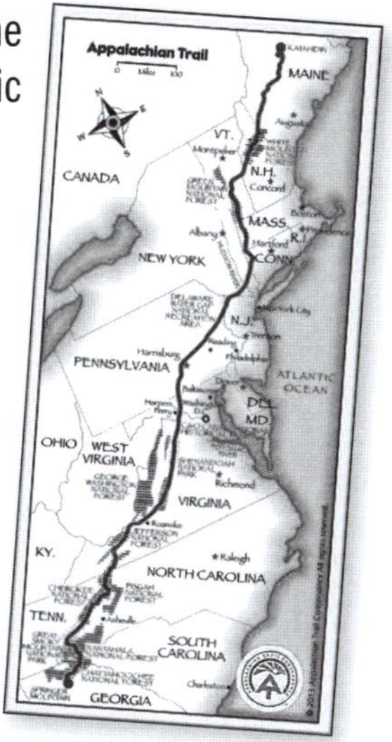

- 2019: Robert Sanchez Jr.: The Iraq War veteran was stabbed to death by a disturbed man who had been threatening people on the trail.
- 1981: Robert Mountford Jr. and Laura Susan Ramsay: The two social workers were hiking the trail to raise money for troubled teenagers when they were murdered. The culprit was caught and served 15 years in prison before returning to the same location years later, where he tried to kill again.
- 1975: Janice Balza: The thru-hiker was killed by a man who wanted her backpack.

Thursday, March 26 2026

TRUE CRIME QUIZ

Serial killer Rodney Alcala appeared on which TV show in 1978?

A. *The Dating Game*

B. *Jeopardy!*

C. *Mork & Mindy*

D. *The $25,000 Pyramid*

Answer: A. Alcala was one of the three bachelors on an episode of *The Dating Game*. He was chosen by the woman for her date. However, she later refused to go out with him, noting that he seemed "creepy." And it's a good thing she did: He had killed his first victim, a 23-year-old flight attendant named Cornelia Crilley, in 1971. By the time he was arrested in 1979, he had murdered seven or more women.

FATAL ATTRACTION

On May 6, 2016, US Customs and Border Protection employee Eddy Reyes called his wife, Claudia, at work to let her know he would be taking her to dinner that night. But after picking her up, instead of going on a date, authorities said he drove them to his mother's garage, where he and his gang member half brother choked her to death, all because Eddy suspected she had cheated on him.

The next day, Eddy reportedly texted one of Claudia's coworkers with her phone claiming she couldn't come to work. A few days later, Eddy filed a missing persons report on Claudia.

Claudia's friends and family did not believe Eddy's story that she had left him for another man, so they decided to get the FBI involved. Soon, they found Claudia's blood in the car Eddy rented the night of the killing. A cadaver dog also indicated that a dead body had been in the vehicle.

Eddy, who had a history of domestic violence against his wife (and had even been served restraining orders in the past), pleaded guilty in 2024 to kidnapping resulting in death.

Saturday, March 28 2026

Sunday, March 29 2026

Palm Sunday

"Out of curiosity."

—The reason given by Jung Yoo-jung, a 23-year-old South Korean true crime fan who confessed to murdering a tutor she sought online

Monday, March 30 2026

These are some of the most popular true crime tourist attractions in the United States:

- The Lizzie Borden House (Fall River, Massachusetts)
- The Clutter House, site of the *In Cold Blood* murders (Holcomb, Kansas)
- The Sowden House, site of the Black Dahlia murder (Los Angeles, California)
- Versace Mansion, site of Gianni Versace's murder (Miami, Florida)

TERMINOLOGY

Dark tourism

Also known in academic circles as *thanatourism*, this is the phenomenon in which people travel in large numbers to locations where terrible things have happened. While dark tourist sites are often pinned to historical or natural tragedies (such as 9/11 or the 79 CE volcanic eruption at Pompeii), they are sometimes also linked to violent crimes (such as the places where some of the Jack the Ripper murders took place in London, or Umberto's Clam House in New York's Little Italy, where mobster "Crazy Joe" Gallo was assassinated in 1972).

Passover begins at sundown

THE YORKSHIRE RIPPER

Part I: Warning Signs

The warning signs around Peter Sutcliffe were flashing long before he started his crime spree. Born in 1946 in Yorkshire, England, he was raised in a chaotic household by a womanizing, heavy drinking, hyperviolent father who smashed a glass on Sutcliffe's head when the boy was just five years old. But given that none of his siblings became serial killers, there may have been something in Sutcliffe's makeup that was scarred from the start.

Bullied, lonely, and awkward, Sutcliffe was painfully miserable in school until finally dropping out at age 15. He worked as a laborer, where coworkers noticed some odd predilections. While working as a gravedigger in the 1960s, he showed a streak of dark humor and fascination with corpses that stood out even in that industry. At some point during his youth, Sutcliffe also developed a habit familiar to many serial killers: attacking sex workers.

Sutcliffe's first attack was in 1969. After hitting a sex worker in the head with a rock, he was questioned by police but, when the woman declined to press charges, he was not arrested.

Thursday, April 2 2026

THE YORKSHIRE RIPPER

Part II: The Ripper Starts

After his first attack in 1969, Peter Sutcliffe waited six years before returning to his dark impulses. On three occasions during the summer of 1975, he used a hammer and knife to attack women walking alone at night. All survived, but were left with severe physical and psychological trauma.

Sutcliffe's first murder victim was Wilma Mary McCann, a 28-year-old mother of four. After he killed her on October 30, 1975, a massive investigation turned up nothing. Over the next five years, Sutcliffe roamed the Yorkshire area, sadistically hunting and murdering women every few months. Media coverage and public panic accelerated, especially when it became clear that not all his victims were sex workers (an attorney general was criticized for saying the "saddest part" of the murders was that some victims had been "totally respectable women"). In 1978, letters started to come to police and the press signed the "Yorkshire Ripper." Although the letters later turned out to be a hoax, the moniker stuck to Sutcliffe.

Ultimately, Sutcliffe was connected to at least 13 murders between 1975 and 1980, with seven more attempted killings.

THE YORKSHIRE RIPPER

Part III: A Botched Investigation

During Peter Sutcliffe's reign of terror across northern England in the 1970s, he was questioned by police a total of nine times, including once after a friend of Sutcliffe's tried to report him as a suspect. Arrested for drunk driving in 1980, he continued his attacks for months while awaiting trial. Sutcliffe murdered two more women and assaulted another two before he was finally arrested.

The Yorkshire Ripper's terror didn't stop until January 2, 1981. Sutcliffe was pulled over by police while driving with a young sex worker in his car, which had false plates. He confessed after a two-day interrogation, though he pleaded not guilty to the 13 murders. According to Sutcliffe, his killings were by the orders of God. The jury didn't buy his claims of divine inspiration or potential schizophrenia and sentenced him to 20 concurrent life sentences.

Sutcliffe died in prison from COVID-19 in 2020.

Saturday, April 4 2026

Sunday, April 5 2026

Easter

TRUE CRIME QUIZ

How many gig drivers were killed on the job between 2017 and 2022?

A. 23

B. 4

C. 50

D. 11

Answer: C. According to the group Gig Workers Rising, 50 drivers were killed in that time span. In one case from 2021, a Lyft driver in Texas was killed by a passenger who had been previously investigated for terrorism and later died in a police shoot-out.

ON THIS DAY

Canadian Bikers Lured to Their Deaths

In the early 2000s, the Bandidos biker gang's Toronto chapter was doing a brisk business in dealing methamphetamine. But trouble loomed. Wayne "Weiner" Kellestine, a Nazi enthusiast and former Bandidos president with a long record of murder accusations, decided to make a dramatic move to put the operation under his control.

On the night of April 7, 2006, Kellestine lured seven Bandidos to his remote farmhouse in London, Ontario. When Luis Manny "Chopper" Raposo heard a noise in the rafters, he looked up to see one of Kellestine's confederates pointing a rifle at him. Three Bandidos were shot and killed instantly. Kellestine attempted to convince the survivors to join him, but after several fruitless hours, they were marched outside one at a time and shot dead in their cars.

Kellestine attempted to pin the eight executions on the Hells Angels, but this plan unraveled almost immediately. (One former Bandido described Kellestine's planning as "meth logic.") Kellestine and five co-conspirators were found guilty of murder in 2009.

THE HORROR BEFORE AMITYVILLE

Of all the "based on a true story" horror tales of the 1970s, *The Amityville Horror* is one of the most frightening. The 1977 book and 1979 movie told the story of the Lutz family, who in December 1975 moved into a charming old Dutch Colonial house at 112 Ocean Avenue, Amityville, on Long Island, only to discover (according to them) that it was infested with demonic spirits.

One of the house's selling points was that it came furnished. In a detail that might have spooked other buyers, the furniture turned out to belong to the previous inhabitants, the DeFeos. About a year earlier, eldest son Ronald DeFeo Jr. had stalked through the house and shot his parents and four siblings to death in their beds.

Less than a month after they moved in, the Lutzes were gone from what became known as the "Amityville House." The house had been a steal. But one can only take so many slamming doors, eerie sounds, spontaneously shattering windows, and disembodied voices hissing, "*Get out*."

Ryan Jenkins

The world of reality TV is filled with fights on-screen. It has also faced murder off-screen.

Ryan Jenkins married swimsuit model Jasmine Fiore in Las Vegas in March 2009 just days after they met. Jenkins was a reality TV performer, having been cut from the show *Megan Wants a Millionaire* not long before meeting Fiore. Just weeks after their wedding, Jenkins was charged with domestic violence. He had also apparently been consumed with jealousy, calling Fiore frequently from the Mexico set of another reality show (*I Love Money 3*) he was filming at the time.

On August 15, 2009, Fiore's body was found. She had been strangled, beaten, and stuffed into a suitcase left in an alley in Buena Park, California. Although Jenkins had reported her missing beforehand, once police tried to get in touch, he went on the run.

Amid the investigation, it was revealed that Jenkins had a Canadian criminal record that included a 2005 arrest for assaulting his girlfriend. Apparently, the reality TV producers he worked with had not uncovered his shady past. *Megan Wants a Millionaire* was soon taken off the air, and Jenkins was found dead from suicide in a British Columbia hotel on August 23, 2009.

WITHOUT A TRACE

Trevaline Evans

Trevaline Evans led a quiet life in Llangollen, Wales. The married mother of one had a passion for antiques, and she pursued her hobby with dedication, opening her own store, Attic Antiques, in 1989. On June 16, 1990, she stepped away from the shop at around 12:40 p.m., leaving a note reading "Back in two minutes." After one sighting at 2:30 p.m., she was never seen again, and her killer, if there was one, was never found.

Although Evans's husband was questioned (unproven rumors suggested she may have fled due to an unhappy marriage), he was released.

The search (the largest in Welsh history at the time) went on for years. But even after unconfirmed sightings in Australia, France, and London; the investigation of serial killer Robin Ligus (one of whose victims was an antiques dealer); and assistance from a spiritualist, Trevaline's body was never recovered.

CRIME STATS
A Bad Way to Go

Professor Austin Sarat's book *Gruesome Spectacles* analyzed executions in America between 1890 and 2010. His research found that of the 8,776 people executed in that time period, roughly 3 percent of the executions, or 276, were carried out improperly.

Sarat broke down the methods by their likelihood of being "botched" (which he described as "a breakdown in, or departure from, the 'protocol' for a particular method of execution," leading to things such as electrocuted convicts catching fire during electrocution, or others slowly strangling during hangings):

- Lethal injection: 7.12 percent
- Lethal gas: 5.4 percent
- Hanging: 3.12 percent
- Electrocution: 1.92 percent
- Firing squad: 0 percent

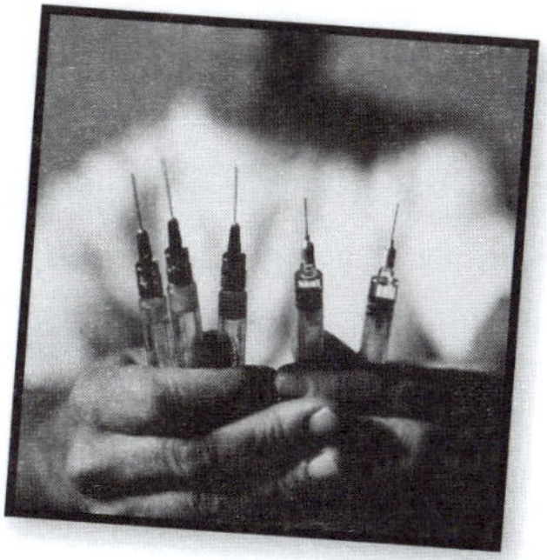

Saturday, April 11 2026

Sunday, April 12 2026

Orthodox Easter

"Get me John Gotti's lawyer."

—Fourteen-year-old "Josephine Bell" (a pseudonym) after being arrested with several other teenagers in Victoria, Canada, for the 1997 murder of 14-year-old Reena Virk

(According to Rebecca Godfrey's book *Under the Bridge*, the arresting officer replied, "I don't think he's available.")

ANDREW CUNANAN

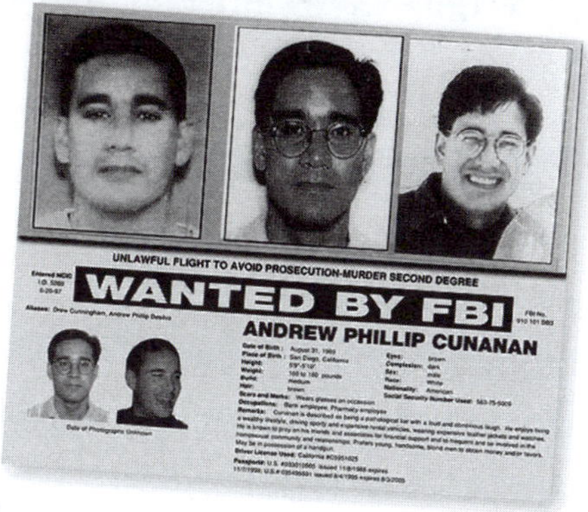

Part I: Summer of '97

Andrew Cunanan had an early reputation as a big talker, which later metastasized into pathological lying. A hustler with a genius IQ of 147 and an aversion to work, Cunanan dropped out of college and moved to San Francisco, California. There, he lived off a string of wealthy male lovers while also dealing drugs to support his excessive spending habits (travel, clothes, clubbing).

By 1996, a 27-year-old Cunanan was struggling to keep his patrons. After an older lover—his main financial supporter—dumped him, Cunanan spiraled. In early 1997, he told friends he was flying to Minnesota so he could "settle some business" with an old friend, Jeff Trail.

Cunanan and Trail had been close friends in San Diego in the early 1990s, while Trail was struggling with being gay in the US Navy, but apparently the two had never been lovers. Cunanan even used to call Trail "my brother." Exhausted by Cunanan's appetite for drama and lies, Trail had since moved to Minneapolis for a job in 1996 and befriended David Madson, an ex-lover of Cunanan's.

Tuesday, April 14 2026

ANDREW CUNANAN

Part II: Minnesota to Miami

Andrew Cunanan's murder spree started in April 1997 in Minneapolis, where he seemed to feel out of options. Apparently upset at how close his friends Jeff Trail and David Madson had become in his absence, the terminally insecure and now financially strained Cunanan lashed out. He beat Trail to death in Madson's apartment on April 27. Nearly a week later, the body of Madson—who may have been held hostage by Cunanan—was found north of the city with multiple gunshot wounds from a handgun Cunanan had taken from Trail.

After that point, Cunanan turned from seeking revenge on people in his life to killings of opportunity. Cunanan drove Madson's Jeep to Chicago and chose Lee Miglin, an older real estate millionaire, as his next victim for reasons unknown. After sadistically butchering Miglin in his garage, Cunanan went into the mogul's mansion, where he ate some ham and had a shower before heading east in Miglin's Lexus.

On May 9, Cunanan shot cemetery caretaker William Reese in a small New Jersey town and stole his pickup truck.

About a month later, Cunanan was on the FBI's Ten Most Wanted list. By then, he was in Miami and looking for his next target.

ANDREW CUNANAN

Part III: The Killer's Last Act

Andrew Cunanan met his final victim only twice before his death: once, in the VIP room of a San Francisco nightclub in 1990, and again, at the San Francisco Opera House. There is little indication Cunanan had seen Italian fashion designer Gianni Versace again before they would meet for a third and final time.

When Cunanan came to Miami in mid-May 1997, he was the subject of a nationwide manhunt. Nevertheless, he somehow managed to move about freely. At one point, he pawned gold coins stolen from Miglin and, although his identification was sent to police, they never followed up.

There are several possible reasons for Cunanan's fixation on Versace, who lived in a gloriously ostentatious South Beach villa. Whatever the cause, Versace did match the profile of the kind of man who had once taken care of Cunanan.

But when Cunanan approached Versace on the steps of his mansion on July 15, 1997, he did not ask for money or try to start a relationship. Instead, Cunanan shot Versace twice in the back of the head, killing him. Eight days later, Cunanan shot himself on a houseboat where he had holed up until it was surrounded by the FBI.

TERMINOLOGY

Suicide by cop

A situation wherein a person facing some kind of mental health crisis engineers a scenario (sometimes but not always after they have harmed or killed someone) in which law enforcement officers have no choice but to shoot them dead.

TRUE CRIME QUIZ

Which of the following is *not* the nickname of a real serial killer?

A. The Lady Killer

B. The Frown-Faced Ripper

C. The Florida Sex Beast

D. Dr. Death

Answer: B. The "Lady Killer" was serial killer Ricardo Silvio Caputo's nickname; the "Florida Sex Beast" was Gerard Schaefer; and "Dr. Death" was Harold Shipman.

BOBBI JO AND JENNIFER

Part I: Losing It in Texas

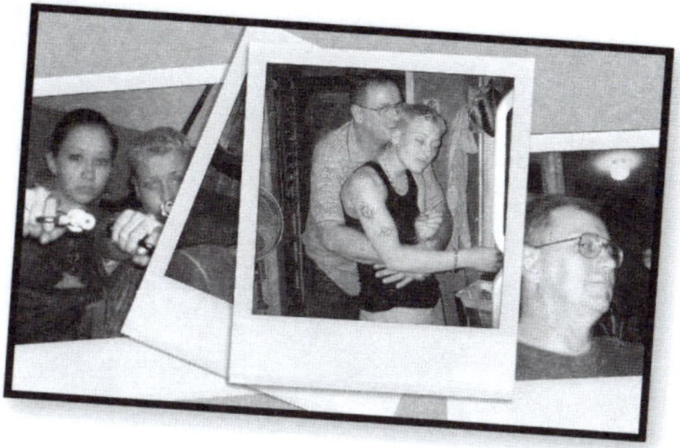

Bobbi Jo Smith, 19, and Jennifer Lynn Jones, 18, were young and in love when they decided to commit murder in 2004.

Living in Mineral Wells, Texas, the two young women were raised in a world of rampant dysfunction, relentless chaos, and few prospects. Jones was stealing, committing fraud, and getting heavily into drugs by the time she was 16. Smith had a knack for getting what she wanted. The two fell in love quickly, right around the time Jones's family life was imploding.

Jones moved in with Smith, who at that time had a 49-year-old roommate, Bob Dow. Smith and Dow had an arrangement: Dow supplied Smith (and later Jones) with drugs and, in exchange, Smith brought young women (and some underaged girls) back to his place for parties, sex, and the occasional amateur porn film.

Following a weeks-long drug binge, Smith and Jones were strung out and hearing voices. After the two were arrested for shoplifting and Dow bailed them out, Dow suggested Jones could pay him back by sleeping with him. Jones and Smith had a different idea.

BOBBI JO AND JENNIFER

Part II: On the Run

Frazzled after three days of binging meth with no food or sleep, Bobby Jo Smith and Jennifer Jones decided that Dow wanting to sleep with Jones was an attempt to break them up. They decided they needed to get rid of him.

On May 5, 2004, Smith gave Jones a .22 handgun. Jones tucked it into her back waistband under her shirt, went to Dow's apartment, and said she had changed her mind. Once in the bedroom, she told him to put a pillow over his face. He was later found dead with three bullet holes in the pillow.

Smith and Jones excitedly told Jones's mother, sister, and her sister's girlfriend about the killing. Then all five took off in Dow's truck, and the motley crew fled westward.

Bit by bit, the thrill-kill couple's companions dropped off. Soon, it was just Smith and Jones heading to the West Coast, where they imagined a new life or a dramatic death in a hail of bullets. Disappointingly for the two, they were arrested without incident and convicted. Jones was sentenced to 48 years in prison, while Smith got 50.

Tuesday, April 21 2026

CRIME INVESTIGATION
Henry Faulds

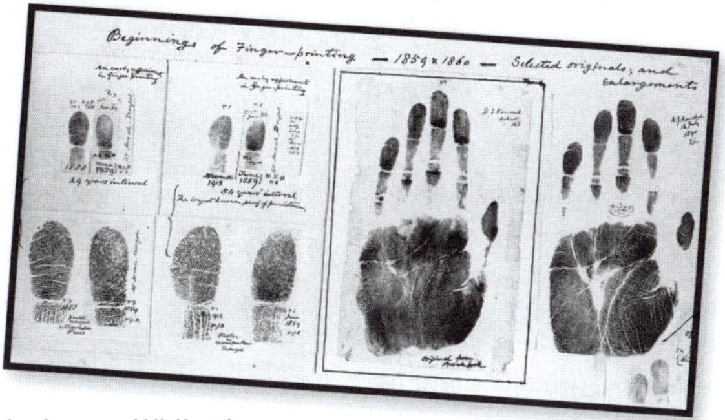

Henry Faulds was a true polymath. The religious Scottish man studied everything from mathematics to the classics, before he eventually took up medicine and, in 1847, established his home country's first medical mission in Japan. While there, the busy Faulds wrote travel books, worked as a surgeon, and opened a hospital before inadvertently revolutionizing the field of criminal investigation.

Faulds was on an archaeological dig with a friend when he noticed the fingerprints left by potters in clay shards. Not long after, his hospital was burglarized. Japanese police arrested a suspect whom Faulds thought was innocent. He helped free the man after comparing his fingerprints to those found at the crime scene.

Using that experience as his jumping-off point, Faulds published an article in *Nature* in 1880 that essentially established the field of forensic fingerprinting. Faulds tried to offer his services to Scotland Yard, but for years, his methods were ignored. It was not until well after his death in 1930 that Faulds was acknowledged for his role in making fingerprinting a part of criminology.

Wednesday, April 22 2026

Earth Day

EXONERATED
Kirk Bloodsworth

On July 25, 1984, the body of a nine-year-old girl was found in a wooded area in Maryland. She had been strangled, raped, and beaten with a rock before her death. After a sketch artist made a composite of a man witnesses had seen walking with the girl, an anonymous tip directed police to Kirk Bloodsworth, a 22-year-old ex-marine living in Baltimore. Even though his appearance differed from descriptions of the man (Bloodsworth was heavy-set and redheaded, while the suspect was said to be skinny and blond), and authorities lacked physical evidence, Bloodsworth was arrested. In 1985, he was sentenced to death after being convicted of rape, sexual assault, and murder.

While imprisoned, Bloodsworth studied the growing field of DNA evidence. In 1992, tests of the victim's clothing showed no match with Bloodsworth. He was released and pardoned in 1993, after almost nine years in prison. Later, he became an advocate for death row exonerees and was a leader in the successful fight to abolish Maryland's death penalty.

Thursday, April 23 2026

Blue box

DIY devices used by so-called "phone phreakers" and proto-hackers in the pre-internet 1960s and 1970s, these gadgets could imitate the tones used by telephone operators to access free long-distance calls. Similar "red boxes" were used to trick pay phones into allowing free calls. Once used by a young Steve Jobs and other future tech titans, the boxes lost their appeal in the 1970s, after AT&T made changes to their switching systems, and famous phone phreaker John Draper, aka "Captain Crunch," served time in federal prison.

TRUE CRIME QUIZ

Which of these serial killers did *not* inspire the "Buffalo Bill" character from Thomas Harris's novel *The Silence of the Lambs*?

1. Ed Gein
2. Gary M. Heidnik
3. Jeffrey Dahmer
4. Ted Bundy

Saturday, April 25 2026

Anzac Day (AUS & NZ)

Sunday, April 26 2026

Answer: 3. Harris used elements of Bundy's, Gein's, and Heidnik's obsessions and methods to fashion the character who FBI agent Clarice Starling kills at the end of the novel.

EXPERTS SAY

A 2019 study found that one of the leading causes of wrongful convictions was the misleading use of forensic science at trial. Among the examples uncovered:

- Bite mark analysis: This widely debunked method has contributed to at least one wrongful murder conviction.
- Touch DNA amplification: Mayer Herskovic was convicted of second-degree assault in 2016 after new software claimed the ability to "amplify" DNA samples that were otherwise too small to use, but he was exonerated once the software was deemed unreliable.
- Microscopic hair comparison: Glenn Payne was convicted of sexually abusing a two-year-old neighbor in part because of an analyst who supposedly found a link between Payne and a hair found at the scene. In 2017, the FBI determined that this method was unreliable, and Payne's conviction was vacated in 2018.

"**The common argument that crime is caused by poverty is a kind of slander on the poor.**"

—H. L. Mencken

JUSTICE DELAYED

Larry Nassar

Larry Nassar was the US women's national gymnastics team doctor for 18 years. Although numerous women under his care made allegations of sexual assault against him, the FBI's lengthy delays allowed Nassar to keep preying on victims until 2016.

At long last, Nassar was brought to trial and in 2018 was sentenced to 40 to 175 years in prison by a judge who told the 54-year-old Nassar, "I just signed your death warrant."

In 2024, the US Department of Justice agreed to a $138.7 million settlement with more than 100 people who had accused the FBI of mishandling the investigation.

THE BOY IN THE BOX

On February 25, 1957, authorities found a large cardboard JCPenney box left in the woods around Philadelphia's Fox Chase neighborhood. Inside, wrapped in a blanket, was the battered, malnourished body of a four-year-old boy.

The resulting investigation around the unknown "Boy in the Box" gained nationwide attention. But despite hundreds of leads, and the work of pioneering forensic anthropologist Wilton Krogman, nothing definitive was ever discovered.

After two exhumations of the body for DNA material and years of work from professional and amateur detectives, the boy's identity was finally discovered in 2022.

Genealogists found that his name was Joseph Augustus Zarelli. Though his parents had died before the time his identity was revealed, authorities say he still had some living siblings.

HEISTS

1981 Brink's Robbery

Moving cash has always been dangerous. Dating back to the early 1900s, banks have relied on armored truck companies, like Brink's, to keep their funds safe.

One of the more infamous and organized armored truck heists was the 1981 Brink's robbery. That October 20, a cohort of heavily armed Black Liberation Army members ambushed a Brink's truck picking up $1.6 million in cash from a bank in New York's Rockland County. As two guards approached the truck with a dolly of cash, the robbers opened fire, killing one and wounding the other.

The robbers drove their van to a nearby rendezvous, where members of the Weather Underground militant group were waiting with a getaway car and truck. When the truck was stopped by police, two officers and one robber were killed in the ensuing furious firefight that sent onlookers running for cover.

All the remaining robbers were eventually found and put on trial.

Friday, May 1 2026

Asian American and Pacific Islander Heritage Month begins (US)

TRUE CRIME QUIZ

Fans of the true crime podcast *My Favorite Murder* have what nickname?

A. Murderinos

B. The Killers

C. Bundyites

D. Sick and Twisteds

Saturday, May 2 2026

Sunday, May 3 2026

Answer: A. "Murderinos" may have been inspired by *The Simpsons*'s Ned Flanders' tendency to append "-ino" to just about anything.

THE O. J. CONFESSION

Part I: Trial of the Century

Nicole Brown Simpson and her friend Ron Goldman were found stabbed to death at her Brentwood home on June 12, 1994. Her ex-husband O. J. Simpson, a football star and beloved celebrity, was the immediate suspect. O. J. Simpson, who had a history of physically and emotionally abusing Nicole Brown Simpson, was soon accused of the murders. Five days after the killings, he even led the police on a slow-speed car chase.

Televised live, the sensational monthslong 1995 trial shocked the country and exposed racial tensions in America. After Simpson was found not guilty, speculation about his guilt swirled even as he continued to protest his innocence.

THE O. J. CONFESSION

Part II: Simpson Agrees to Talk

The book that Judith Regan agreed to publish was not actually written by O. J. Simpson, but a ghostwriter who interviewed him. This was not unusual. What *was* unusual was the topic of the book itself.

Titled *If I Did It: Confessions of the Killer*, the book was presented as an imaginary presentation of how Simpson *might* have killed Nicole Brown Simpson and Ron Goldman. When ABC and Barbara Walters pulled out of the advance publicity for the book, following criticism, Regan decided to conduct a five-hour interview with Simpson to promote the book. While insisting everything he said was "hypothetical," Simpson explained in fine detail all that led up to the killings, but then claimed not to remember what actually happened.

Regan later told the *New York Times* that Simpson "hangs himself with every word" of the interview. "His basic view was that she had it coming. He saw himself as a victim."

Part III: No Book

Unsurprisingly, when word got out that O. J. Simpson was about to release a book that could generate a lot of money, the controversy was electric. Even though the publisher had agreed to put any revenue from the book into trusts for Simpson's children with Nicole Brown Simpson, the publication was canceled.

The Goldman family had won a lawful death lawsuit against Simpson in 1997 for $33.5 million. After winning the rights to *If I Did It*, the Goldmans published it in 2007 with a new afterword by investigative journalist Dominick Dunne, which stated his belief in Simpson's guilt.

By the time Simpson died of cancer in 2024, interest had swelled his debt to the Goldmans to more than $100 million. Ultimately, proceeds from the book were the only money the Goldman family ever received.

DID O. J. DO IT?

When O. J. Simpson was acquitted of murder in 1995, public beliefs about his culpability were drawn starkly between Black and white Americans. It is still divided but less so:

- In 1997, 82 percent of white Americans thought Simpson was guilty, and 31 percent of Black Americans agreed.
- By 2015, the percentage of white Americans believing in Simpson's guilt was unchanged at 83 percent. But the percentage of Black Americans believing in his guilt had nearly doubled to 57 percent.

"Singularity is almost invariably a clue. The more featureless and commonplace a crime is, the more difficult is it to bring it home."

—Sherlock Holmes in Arthur Conan Doyle's "The Boscombe Valley Mystery," *The Adventures of Sherlock Holmes*

Friday, May 8 2026

TRUE CRIME QUIZ

The 1966 Supreme Court ruling *Miranda v. Arizona* created guidelines for law enforcement to follow to ensure detained suspects understand their constitutional rights. Answer the following questions about "Miranda Rights," true or false:

1. If your rights aren't read to you after being arrested, your case is automatically thrown out.
2. A full 80 percent of arrestees waive their right to remain silent.
3. Nothing you say to the police before being taken into custody can be used in court.
4. Each state can decide how to word their Miranda warnings.

Saturday, May 9 2026

Sunday, May 10 2026

Mother's Day

Answer: 1: False. **2:** True. **3:** False. **4:** True.

TERMINOLOGY

Family annihilator

A specific variant of mass murderer (nearly always a man) who kills their children, then spouse, and then themselves. Sometimes the killings are motivated by family breakdowns or financial distress. Other times, the killer is operating under the false belief that they are somehow protecting their family.

COUNTERFEITING

Part I

Instead of robbing stores or stealing from banks, some criminals just make whatever they want. Anybody who has purchased a supposedly brand-name purse from a sidewalk vendor at a fraction of the usual cost has almost definitely bought a fake. There are entire factories devoted to turning out products made to look like the "real" thing so they can be resold. Some experts have estimated that the fake goods market is worth between $1.5 and $4.5 trillion, making counterfeits larger than most nations' economies.

Tuesday, May 12 2026

COUNTERFEITING

Part II

The most popular counterfeited goods on the black market include:

- Apple AirPods
- Chanel perfume
- Gucci bags
- Louis Vuitton bags
- Burberry apparel

"Crime isn't a disease, it's a symptom. Cops are like a doctor that gives you aspirin for a brain tumor, except that the cop would rather cure it with a blackjack. . . . Organized crime is just the dirty side of the sharp dollar."

—Philip Marlowe in Raymond Chandler's *The Long Goodbye*

Thursday, May 14 2026

TRUE CRIME QUIZ

Serial killer Henry Louis Wallace was sometimes known as the "_______ Strangler." What is the missing word or phrase?

A. Taco Bell

B. Applebee's

C. Wendy's

D. White Castle

Answer: A. Wallace, who confessed to killing 11 women in Charlotte, North Carolina, between 1990 and 1994, was called the "Taco Bell Strangler" because he had been a manager at a Taco Bell and tended to get to know his victims while working at various fast food restaurants.

CRIME STATS

Places Not to Commit Crimes

Nobody wants to go to prison. But if you're imprisoned, some are worse than others. Here are the five states with the highest mortality rates in their prison populations (per 100,000 prisoners) as of 2022:

1. Louisiana: 687
2. Alabama: 588*
3. Mississippi: 544
4. Tennessee: 532
5. Kentucky: 516

***Alabama also had the highest number of homicides, with 63 out of a prison population of about 22,000.**

Saturday, May 16 2026

Sunday, May 17 2026

THE PILLOW PYRO

Part I: The Pasadena Blaze

On the evening of October 10, 1984, an alarm went off at Ole's Home Center hardware store in South Pasadena. A fire had started and quickly spread. Two employees and two customers (a grandmother and her two-year-old grandson) were killed. The cause was determined to be an electrical fire, though one of the fire investigators, John Leonard Orr, insisted it was arson.

In 1987, a California fire investigators convention was held in the city of Fresno. Around the time of the convention, a series of fires broke out in the vicinity of nearby Bakersfield. Nobody was hurt, but one investigator, Captain Martin Casey, noticed the flammable devices used to start the blazes had been tucked into pillows. It reminded him of the South Pasadena fire from 1984, which he thought had been arson and made him think the suspect was an arson investigator like himself.

Two more series of fires followed—in 1989 near Pacific Grove and in Los Angeles in 1990—with similar patterns. A "Pillow Pyro" task force was established, and Casey was given permission to test a partial fingerprint found at one of the 1987 fires. As Casey suspected, it matched one of his comrades.

Part II: Investigating the Investigator

John Leonard Orr, aka the "Pillow Pyro," had originally wanted to be a police officer. But after failing the psychological test, he joined the fire department instead and became an arson investigator. Though he was generally well-liked, he was also known for his strange knack for being the first one to show up at suspicious fires.

In 1991, the Pillow Pyro task force had matched Orr to one of the nonfatal blazes and followed him by putting a tracking device on his car. A search of his home revealed videotapes of burning buildings and fire-setting materials that matched those used to set the fires.

After Orr was arrested on December 4, 1991, the number of large-scale fires in Southern California plummeted.

Found guilty of four counts of first-degree murder for the 1984 Ole's Home Center fire in 1998, Orr was given multiple life sentences without parole.

THE PILLOW PYRO

Part III: Stranger Than Fiction

John Leonard Orr craved attention and wanted recognition for his work. Even though he was connected to roughly 2,000 fires set in California between 1984 and 1991, he didn't believe his role as a firestarter had been properly acknowledged, so he wrote a book about it. The never-published *Points of Origin* was about a fictional arson investigator named Aaron Stiles, who moonlights as an arsonist. In the book, Orr describes Stiles's reaction to the fires he sets: "The smoke was beautiful, causing his heart rate to quicken and his breathing to come in shallow gasps."

Though Orr—who had psychopathic traits—was prolific, he was by no means one of a kind. In the 1990s, fire departments collaborated with the FBI to develop tests to screen out potential arsonists among their new hires, and the number of firefighters arrested for arson dropped from about 40 to 3 per year.

TERMINOLOGY

Pyrophilia

Sometimes confused with the more common *pyromania*, a person with *pyrophilia* not only enjoys setting fires but can also find sexual gratification in doing so. “Pillow Pyro” John Leonard Orr is one of the most famous pyrophiliacs.

CAUGHT BY BLOOD

Colin Pitchfork

In 1986, police in Leicestershire, England, launched an unprecedented investigation. Locals were terrified of a killer who had raped and strangled two 15-year-old girls in identical fashion in the same location: one in 1983 and the other in 1986. A geneticist at the nearby University of Leicester had recently made a breakthrough in DNA fingerprinting, a process that had not yet been used to identify criminal suspects. Deciding now was the time, police requested blood samples from every local man between the ages of 16 and 34.

Thousands complied. But Colin Pitchfork, a 27-year-old baker and father of two, manipulated a friend into taking the test for him. After the friend confessed, Pitchfork was arrested, and police took a blood sample that linked him not only to both murders, but two additional rapes.

The first murderer to be convicted by DNA, Pitchfork was asked why he had killed the second girl. “Opportunity,” he shrugged. “She was there and I was there.”

HUSBAND REMOVAL SERVICE

In late 19th-century Russia, many poor women often had to endure abusive husbands for years with no possible recourse. There were some, however, who were fortunate enough to come across a helpful neighbor: Madame Alexe Katherina Popova. A native of the southwestern city of Samara, Madame Popova had survived her own abusive marriage and came to offer her services to other women suffering from domestic violence: For a reasonable fee, Popova would eliminate the husband by various means, most commonly with arsenic.

Popova ran her "business" for decades until one of her customers felt a pang of guilt and turned her in. When she was arrested in 1909, Popova proudly admitted to "freeing" roughly 300 "unhappy wives from their tyrants."

Despite the efforts of a furious mob that wanted to burn her at the stake, soldiers kept Popova alive just long enough for her to be found guilty and executed by firing squad.

WALK OF DEATH

Part I: Trained for Killing

Howard Unruh joined the US Army in 1942 at the age of 21 at the height of World War II. From 1944 to 1945, he battled his way across Europe and kept disturbing, detailed notes on every German he killed. After returning to the States as a veteran, he was directionless and angry at the world. He lived with his mother, bouncing from one job to the next and developing a significant persecution complex. Then, on the morning of September 6, 1949, he took his Luger pistol, a war souvenir, and went looking for people he thought had "talked about him."

Unruh walked through his Camden, New Jersey, neighborhood and began shooting his targets. Within just 20 minutes, he had killed 3 children and 10 adults. Unruh showed no emotion during his rampage, which became known as the "Walk of Death."

By the time police arrived, Unruh was back in his apartment.

WALK OF DEATH

Part II: The Showdown

Following Unrah's 20-minute shooting spree, he holed up in his apartment. Dozens of police officers surrounded the building. They directed a barrage of rifle and machine-gun fire at the apartment and threw tear gas shells through the windows.

While this was going on, local journalist Philip Buxton found Unrah's phone number in a directory and called him. When Unrah picked up, Buxton asked him about "what they're doing to you." Unrah replied, "They're not doing a damned thing to me, but I'm doing plenty to them." When Buxton asked how many people had been killed, Unrah said he didn't know yet "but it looks like a pretty good score." After telling Buxton he couldn't say why he had gone on the rampage, Unrah hung up.

Eventually, Unrah surrendered. After psychiatric testing, he was determined to have paranoid schizophrenia. He was committed to a maximum-security psychiatric facility where he died in 2009.

Corpus delicti

Body of a murder victim. Literal translation from the Latin means “body of the crime.”

“When you have to kill a man it costs nothing to be polite.”

—Winston Churchill

Thursday, May 28 2026

SERIAL KILLERS

A Ranking

When it comes to documented serial killers, the United States far and away leads the world at 3,615. Why? The answer is unclear.

In any case, here is a ranking of the five countries that produced the next-highest numbers of known serial killers, as of 2024:

1. United States: 3,615
2. Russia: 196
3. United Kingdom: 190
4. Japan: 137
5. South Africa: 123
6. India: 121

THE FALCONE KILLING

For years, the Sicilian Mafia, or Cosa Nostra, operated with impunity. Throughout the late 1970s and early 1980s, the group murdered judges and police investigating their heroin-smuggling operations. At the same time, courageous magistrate Giovanni Falcone embarked on a yearslong series of massively complex trials that began to seriously threaten Cosa Nostra's existence. At the end of the enormous Maxi Trial in 1987, Falcone won convictions for 338 out of the 475 defendants.

Falcone's crusade came to an end on May 23, 1992. Early that morning, as Falcone drove near Palermo, Sicily, a 1,100-pound bomb planted by the Cosa Nostra under the roadway exploded. Falcone, his wife, and three police guards were killed. The blast was so powerful it was picked up by scientists studying volcanic tremors at Mount Etna on the opposite end of the island.

Although tragic, the assassination led to an overwhelming show of force by Italian authorities, who spent the next several years systematically dismantling the Cosa Nostra's leadership.

Saturday, May 30 2026

Sunday, May 31 2026

REAL URBAN LEGENDS

The Phrogger

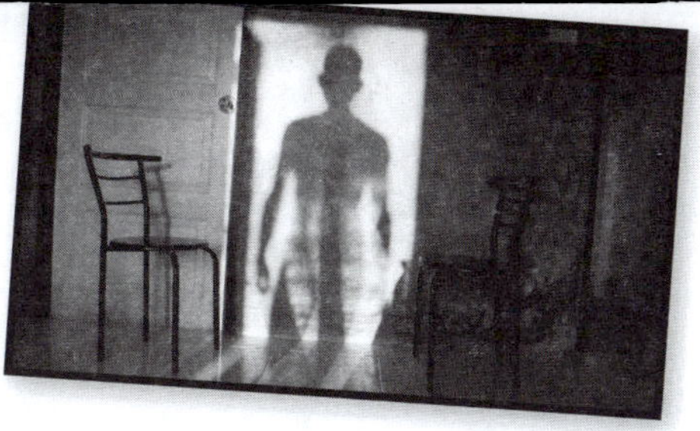

Have you ever heard of a stranger living in someone's home without their knowledge? If so, that person was engaging in something called "phrogging."

In 1987, Townsend, Massachusetts, teenager Daniel LaPlante became obsessed with another local teenager, Tina Bowen. LaPlante started sneaking into Bowen's home and hiding in a secret space inside the walls. At first, he played pranks on Bowen: making noises and moving things when no one was looking. But his stalking escalated suddenly, and one day, a hatchet-wielding LaPlante took Bowen, her sister, father, and a friend hostage. Tina Bowen was able to escape and get help. LaPlante ran away, but a few days later, he returned to spy on Bowen once again. Her father called the police, and he was arrested.

Two months later, while out on bail, LaPlante committed another home invasion with deadly consequences: He raped a woman and then murdered her and her two young children. He was convicted of the murders and was given three consecutive life sentences.

“A bulletproof vest.”

—Convicted murderer James W. Rodgers, when asked if he had a last request while facing his firing squad in 1960

THE MACHETE MURDERER

Part I: A Secret Graveyard

A peach farmer working in his orchards near Yuba City, California, on May 19, 1971, saw a strange, freshly dug hole in the ground. Later in the day, he found it filled in. He called the police, who soon found the freshly buried body of Kenneth Whitacre, killed by a stab wound to the chest and a grievous head injury. Then they found another grave in the orchard. And another. And another. Days later, the police had 25 corpses with stab wounds and heads slashed open, except one victim, who had been shot.

Unlike many serial killer cases, this one was extremely easy to solve. Police found several receipts and deposit slips in the shallow graves with the name "Juan Corona." Searching Corona's house, authorities found a ledger where several of the victims' names were written, a meat cleaver, and a blood-stained machete.

On May 26, just one week after the first body was dug up, Corona was under arrest.

THE MACHETE MURDERER

Part II: Breaking from Reality

Around 1950, decades before he was dubbed the "Machete Murderer," a teenaged Juan Corona crossed into the United States from his native Mexico. He started out as a farm laborer before becoming a labor contractor, essentially hiring other workers for ranches and farms to do the work he once did.

Over the years, Corona had endured multiple periods of mental instability marked by violence and detachment from reality. Following a terrifying 1955 flood that killed dozens of people in Sutter County, California, Corona became convinced ghosts were following him. In 1956, he was hospitalized for schizophrenia. In 1970, he was institutionalized again. Things seemed to come to a head in 1971, when his business was failing and his welfare application was denied.

Corona started his killing spree in February 1971. Picking up a series of migrant workers with no relatives in the area, he murdered them one by one. The murders came to an end in May when Corona's employer, the peach grower who had hired him to supply workers, discovered the victims' graves in his orchard.

THE MACHETE MURDERER

Part III: The Prosecution That Couldn't Prosecute Straight

The trial of Juan Corona should have been an open-and-shut affair. Directly tied to 25 murders through a mountain of evidence, he was put on trial in September 1972.

From the start, however, the prosecution seemed to do everything wrong, including mishandling evidence. The judge declared "the investigation was inept, the preparation inefficient, and the prosecution inadequate."

Though Corona was sentenced to life imprisonment in 1973, a state appellate court overturned the conviction in 1978 on the grounds of an incompetent defense. Corona returned to court in 1982 for a controversially expensive seven-month trial in which one of his lawyers insisted the real killer was Juan's brother, Natividad Corona, on the grounds that he was "an aggressive homosexual."

Juan Corona was again convicted of 25 murders. He didn't admit his guilt until 2011. Even then, he was unclear about whether he felt any remorse or had any motive for the killings.

"So I went and buy the machete and then okay, I started killing when I had to kill all those persons, one by one."

—"Machete Murderer" Juan Corona, asked at his 2011 parole hearing if he had remorse for his actions

Saturday, June 6 2026

Sunday, June 7 2026

CRIME STATS
Female Serial Killers

Michael and C. L. Kelleher's 1998 book *Murder Most Rare: The Female Serial Killer* breaks this uncommon but very real breed of murderer down into nine distinct types: black widow, angel of death, sexual predator, revenge, profit or crime, team killer, question of sanity, unexplained, explained.

TERMINOLOGY

Civil asset forfeiture

This is the practice by which US police are given broad latitude to seize property they believe has anything to do with a crime. This practice does not depend on the owner being arrested or even convicted: It is most commonly used when police departments take cash, cars, or real estate they claim to believe are being used to transport drugs. Because the process of getting the property back is so onerous, many people do not bother in the end.

SCHOOL OF CRIME

During the mid-1930s, Alvin "Creepy" Karpis (pictured on the right of photo) was one of the most wanted men in America. Originally from Montreal, Canada, he was a hardcore burglar and soon got himself a 10-year stint in prison. After escaping in 1930, Karpis hooked up with the Barker family criminal gang. For the next several years, they blazed a trail of crime across the American heartland that included bank robberies, high-profile kidnappings, and murder. The FBI finally grabbed Karpis in 1936 and sentenced him to life in prison.

In the early 1960s, following a long stint at Alcatraz, Karpis was locked up at Washington State's McNeil Island Penitentiary. That's where he met a young offender serving time for forgery and theft. He decided to take the kid under his wing, teaching him guitar and offering life advice.

The kid, whom Karpis had nicknamed "Little Charlie" Manson, never did get his break in the music business. Years later, he would send his cult of followers on a murderous rampage.

JACK THE RIPPER IN NEW YORK CITY

In the 1890s, one of the many colorful characters boozing around New York City was Carrie Brown. An actress in her late 50s, she had been nicknamed "Old Shakespeare" because whenever she got a drink in her, she would perform soliloquies from the Bard's plays and talk about her time as a celebrated actress in England.

Brown was found murdered in her East River Hotel room on April 24, 1891. She had been strangled, disemboweled, and left with an "x" carved into her backside similar to one notched on the wall. The brutal manner of the killing made some people immediately think of Jack the Ripper, who had committed similar murders in London just three years prior.

Newspapers ran with the rumor, one even using the headline "OUR JACK THE RIPPER." Soon people were claiming to see him all around the city, and arrestees were regularly considered as possible Ripper candidates before the mania finally blew over.

TRUE CRIME QUIZ

The “Killer of Oise” stalked northern France from 1978 to 1979. He ran down some young women with his car and shot others. When the killer, Alain Lamare, was finally apprehended, what turned out to be his occupation?

A. Judge

B. Politician

C. Police officer

D. Priest

Answer: C. Lamare was in fact one of the officers involved in the investigation of his own crimes.

LUCAS'S MURDER MAP

Serial killer Henry Lee Lucas liked to dispose of his victims along the stretch of I-35 that ran between Gainesville and Laredo, Texas. As a result, some took to calling that route the "Henry Lee Lucas Memorial Highway."

Saturday, June 13 2026

Sunday, June 14 2026

Flag Day (US)

CRIME STATS

Everyone's Guilty

Some people charged with a crime feel that the deck is stacked against them from the beginning. In China, this may actually be the case. In 2024, the conviction rate of people charged with crimes was over 99 percent. Not to be outdone, one court in Zhejiang province managed an astounding 100 percent conviction over a five-year period in the 1990s.

TERMINOLOGY

CODIS

The Combined DNA Index System (CODIS) is a US national database launched in 1990 as a coordinated effort by multiple crime labs who wanted a central repository to warehouse, share, and compare genetic profiles of criminal suspects and victims. It is currently operated by the FBI.

BLOODS VS. MAFIA

Part I: Fighting over Territory

Sylvester Zottola was not just a Bronx, New York, real estate mogul with millions of dollars in properties under his control; he was also rumored to have ties to the Bonanno crime family. So when he was shot to death in his car at a McDonald's drive-through in October 2018, people may have originally assumed this was part of a Mafia war. It turned out to be a different kind of family conflict.

Sylvester's son, Anthony, had helped him for years with part of the Zottola business: servicing Mafia-controlled gambling machines. At some point, things went south between the two and Anthony started jockeying for control of his father's properties. In an unusual twist, Anthony hired Bushawn Shelton, a leader in the Bloods street gang, to assemble a team of potential assassins who could take out Anthony's father.

BLOODS VS. MAFIA

Part II: Try, Try Again

Anthony Zottola's plot to hire hitmen who could kill his father, Sylvester, did not initially go according to plan. His Bloods associate Bushawn Shelton brought in several attackers to do the deed, but they repeatedly failed, before finally killing Sylvester in October 2018.

- September 2017: An attacker knocked Sylvester to the ground outside his residence.
- November 2017: A masked person tried to shoot Sylvester while driving on the Throgs Neck Expressway.
- December 2017: During a nonfatal home invasion, three attackers hit Sylvester with a gun and stabbed him several times.
- June 2018: A hooded attacker pointed a gun to Sylvester's head but the gun misfired. Sylvester pulled out his own gun and shot back. The attacker escaped.
- July 2018: Sylvester's other son, Salvatore, was shot three times in front of his residence by an attacker; Salvatore survived.

"He who wishes to be rich in a day will be hanged in a year."

—Leonardo da Vinci

Friday, June 19 2026

Juneteenth (US)

ON THIS DAY
Ruth Ellis

Born in 1926 in Wales, Ruth Ellis spent the 1940s working odd jobs in the nightlife industry. She worked her way up to becoming manager of a swinging nightclub in London. Ellis soon fell into a messy affair with David Blakely, a fast-living and hard-drinking racecar driver who was already engaged to another woman. Their relationship was contentious and abusive: At one point, Ellis miscarried after Blakely punched her in the stomach.

On Easter Sunday 1955, Ellis waited outside a pub for Blakely. When he came out, she shot him multiple times with a .38 revolver, killing him.

Ellis was quickly charged with murder, and her trial was a media sensation. She appeared in court on June 20, 1955, dressed and coiffed to the nines. Ellis openly admitted her desire to kill Blakely. Found guilty, she was sentenced to death and executed by hanging on July 13, 1955, at the age of 28. This made Ellis the last woman executed for murder in Great Britain. Although Ellis's guilt was not in question, the public had an overwhelmingly negative reaction to her execution: Thousands signed petitions protesting her punishment, which likely contributed to the government's decision to abolish the death penalty.

Saturday, June 20 2026

Sunday, June 21 2026

Father's Day (US, CAN, UK)

HEISTS

Dunbar Armored Robbery

Part I

On September 12, 1997, Allen Pace III was fired from the Dunbar armored truck depot in downtown Los Angeles for tampering with vehicles. What the company did not know was that Pace was already planning to rob the place in what would become the biggest heist in the city's history.

Having been safety inspector, Pace was well acquainted with the building's security. He recruited five friends and supplied them with weapons, radios, keys, and floor plans. For an alibi, they briefly went to a party together.

The masked and armed robbers entered the depot after midnight on September 13, when Pace knew cash was being sorted for distribution to ATMs. They tied up workers, cut open the vaults with bolt cutters, threw the cash into a rented U-Haul truck, and drove off, returning to the party after changing clothes.

The gang played it cool, carefully laundering the money. They went unnoticed until 1999, when one failed to take the wrappers off stolen cash he used to pay a friend, a real estate broker, who went to the police. Upon arrest, Hill spilled the names of his co-conspirators.

Part II

The 1997 Dunbar heist was one of the biggest, most audacious robberies in Los Angeles history. Some stats on the infamous case include:

- Amount of haul: $18.9 million
- Amount still missing: approx. $10 million
- Time elapsed: 30 minutes
- Shots fired: zero

CRIME DATA

Handguns are the most commonly used weapons when carrying out murders; they are used in roughly 46 percent of all known cases in the United States. Some of the less common means of homicide seen in the US out of a total 13,927 cases recorded by FBI data in 2019 include:

- Blunt objects (clubs, hammers): 397
- Asphyxiation: 92
- Fire: 81
- Strangulation: 64
- Poison: 16

THE VAMPIRE OF SACRAMENTO

Part I: An Obsession with Blood

Born in Sacramento in 1950, Richard Chase was an unusual and unhappy child. A hypochondriac with a tenuous grip on reality (he believed people had stolen his pulmonary artery), he also frequently tortured animals. While many serial killers disembowel small animals in childhood, Chase gave his habits an unusual twist: He would sometimes eat the animals, mixing them with Coca-Cola in a blender.

As Chase grew into his adolescence, his hypochondria and delusional thinking became more advanced. He became increasingly paranoid and obsessed with blood, accelerated by his growing appetites for alcohol and LSD. By 1976, he had been institutionalized for paranoid schizophrenia after killing a rabbit and trying to inject himself with its blood. Unsurprisingly, orderlies called him "Dracula."

Though Chase did not seem to be any variation of "balanced" or "healed," he was eventually released into the care of his mother. Soon she was unable to handle living with him and got him his own apartment. Other tenants didn't like having him around, either. They had good reason.

THE VAMPIRE OF SACRAMENTO

Part II: From Random to Organized

Richard Chase's first known murder appears to have been an unplanned attack. Angry at his mother, Chase was driving past Ambrose Griffin as the married father of two was unloading groceries from his car. Chase shot him dead with a pistol.

Following that somewhat random killing, Chase shifted into a more predatory home invasion mode. To his thinking, unlocked doors were an invitation to kill (he later told an FBI agent that a locked door "means you're not welcome"). After burglarizing a house on January 23, 1978, he was discovered and ran to another home nearby. There, he shot and stabbed to death Teresa Wallin, a young expectant mother. After killing Wallin, Chase gutted her corpse and drank her blood.

Four days later, Chase entered another unlocked house. There, he murdered Evelyn Miroth, Dan Meredith (a friend of Miroth's), her 6-year-old son, and her 22-month-old nephew. He cut apart, partially ate, and had sex with Miroth's brutalized corpse, before escaping with the nephew's body.

Based on descriptions from neighbors and a former classmate of Chase's who was spooked after being approached by him in a store, police arrested him.

Friday, June 26 2026

THE VAMPIRE OF SACRAMENTO

Part III: The Bloody Lair

The trial of Richard Chase started on January 2, 1979, about a year after his last killings.

He seemed to have made little attempt to cover his tracks, being so consumed by his mania for blood and cannibalism. When police searched Chase's apartment, they found an abattoir. Most of the room's surfaces were bloodstained, with horrible smells coming from the blender, and pieces of bone and brain tissue scattered around. Multiple pet collars but no pets in sight suggested he had not only been killing humans. Several weeks later, they found the decapitated body of Evelyn Miroth's nephew.

After five months of grisly testimony in which the prosecution pointed to his premeditation as a sign of a sane mind, Chase was found guilty of six counts of first-degree murder.

Sentenced to death at San Quentin, Chase unnerved his fellow inmates, who urged him to kill himself. The day after Christmas in 1980, he followed their advice by taking an overdose of his antianxiety medication.

"Everyone is a potential suspect, and don't let looks or behavior fool you."

—John E. Douglas and Mark Olshaker, *The Killer Across the Table: Unlocking the Secrets of Serial Killers and Predators with the FBI's Original Mindhunter*

Monday, June 29 2026

TRUE CRIME QUIZ

Where was Natalee Holloway when she went missing?

A. Bermuda

B. Aruba

C. Cuba

D. Puerto Rico

Answer: B. Holloway was last seen getting into a car with Dutch student Joran van der Sloot, outside a nightclub in Oranjestad, Aruba, on the night of May 30, 2005. The 18-year-old Alabama high school graduate's disappearance became an international media sensation.

HEISTS

The Vermeer

Sometime after 9:00 p.m. on April 26, 1974, Sir Alfred Beit and his wife, Lady Clementine Beit, were listening to records in Russborough House, their sprawling villa near Dublin, Ireland. After their servant answered the doorbell, three masked men with assault rifles and a woman stormed in. The thieves tied up the Beits and their staff before focusing on the home's art collection. They made off with 19 works valued today at about $110 million, including paintings by Goya and Rubens, and Vermeer's *Woman Writing a Letter, With Her Maid*.

These were no ordinary thieves. One week later, the Beits received an unsigned letter demanding the release of four convicted Irish Republican Army (IRA) prisoners and a £500,000 (about US $650,000 at the time) ransom; otherwise the paintings would be destroyed.

On May 4, Rose Dugdale, the woman who had accompanied the robbers and pointed out what to steal, was arrested. A rebellious English heiress, Dugdale had spent the last several years immersed in revolutionary politics before committing herself to the IRA's campaign to fight English imperialism. Dugdale served six years in prison. She was unrepentant and continued working for the IRA as a bomb maker.

THE MURDER OF IANA KASIAN

On May 26, 2016, Olga Kasian, a Ukrainian immigrant living in Los Angeles, contacted authorities to carry out a welfare check on her 30-year-old daughter, Iana Kasian. Police found Kasian's 35-year-old boyfriend, Blake Leibel, barricaded inside her West Hollywood apartment along with her body.

The murder had been brutal. The coroner's office believed she had likely been slowly tortured to death over a period of eight hours. Leibel appeared to have bitten and beaten Kasian, tearing off her scalp and parts of her face. By the time Kasian was discovered, Leibel had also completely drained her body of blood.

Son of a wealthy Toronto real estate tycoon, Leibel lived off an $18,000-a-month allowance while balancing several romantic relationships and trying to break into the movie and comics industry. Leibel had published a graphic novel about a vicious killer who drained characters of their blood, and during the trial, prosecutors used his drawings to prove he had planned Kasian's killing. Leibel was sentenced to life without parole in 2018.

"I have never seen this before. And I doubt hardly any forensic pathologists in this country or abroad have even seen this, outside of, perhaps, wartime . . . it's extremely rare."

—Los Angeles coroner Dr. James Ribe describing the torture and mutilation of Iana Kasian by Blake Leibel

Friday, July 3 2026

REAL URBAN LEGENDS

Corpse Under the Bed

In 2003, a guest staying at the Capri Motel near downtown Kansas City, Missouri, complained to management about a strange smell coming from his room. His complaints were repeatedly ignored. After three days, he couldn't take the odor anymore and checked out.

When staff went to clean the room, they lifted the mattress and found the source of the rank odor: a decomposing body.

It does not appear that anyone was ever charged in the death; to this day, it is unknown whether the deceased had climbed under the bed to die by suicide or whether he was murdered.

The motel was torn down several years later, and the sordid tale has become a piece of Kansas City folklore.

Saturday, July 4 2026 Independence Day (US)

Sunday, July 5 2026

GHOSTLY EVIDENCE

The Murder of Zona Heaster Shue

An unusual legal precedent was established in West Virginia in 1897. That January in Greenbriar County, Erasmus Stribbling Trout Shue was working in his blacksmith shop. He asked a boy to go to his home and ask his wife, Elva Zona Heaster Shue, if she needed anything from the store. The boy soon ran back, telling Erasmus he had found Elva dead. After a doctor arrived and tried to resuscitate her, Erasmus asked him to stop. Elva was buried in a high-necked dress.

Not long after, Elva's mother, Mary J. Heaster, announced Elva's ghost had told her the death was a murder, saying "her neck was squeezed off at the first joint." The body was exhumed and a postmortem examination discovered she had a broken neck and crushed windpipe: Elva had likely died from strangulation.

Erasmus was found guilty of Elva's murder, making this the first (and so far only) time a ghost's testimony has led to a conviction.

"Please tell the media, I did not get my Spaghetti-Os. I got spaghetti. I want the press to know."

—Thomas Grasso, just before his execution on March 20, 1995, for the murder of two people, including an 87-year-old woman he strangled to death with her Christmas tree lights

TERMINOLOGY

ViCAP

The Violence Criminal Apprehension Program is an FBI database packed with potentially useful (for authorities, at least) information about homicides and other violent crimes contributed by local police departments.

THE GAY VILLAGE KILLER

For years, Bruce McArthur could be found chatting people up at Zipperz, a bar in Toronto's Gay Village neighborhood. With his belly and white beard, he bore enough of a resemblance to Santa Claus to have once worked as a mall Santa. At the same time, people in the community were concerned about the number of men who had gone missing, worried there was a serial killer in their midst. Police opened an investigation in 2012, but it produced no leads.

In January 2018, bodies were found on land owned by one of McArthur's landscaping clients, and he was soon arrested. He pleaded guilty to killing eight men between 2010 and 2017, many of them Middle Eastern or South Asian immigrants who had not disclosed their sexual identity to their families. McArthur had been involved in a relationship with at least one of the dead, Andrew Kinsman, whose June 2017 disappearance led to increased pressure on police and the start of a second task force.

Up until a few weeks before McArthur's arrest, Toronto police still believed there was no serial killer.

TRUE CRIME QUIZ

Which of these movies did serial killer Ed Gein *not* inspire?

A. *Psycho*

B. *The Texas Chainsaw Massacre*

C. *Monster*

D. *The Silence of the Lambs*

Answer: C. The 2005 film *Monster* was based on sex worker and murderer Aileen Wuornos.

"It might have caused him to reflect (for he was a reflective man, in his own way) on murder's similarity to Lay's potato chips: it's hard to stop with just one."

—*Under the Dome*, Stephen King

Saturday, July 11 2026

Sunday, July 12 2026

CRIME DATA
Reading

Prison leaves a lot of time for working out, gambling, and fighting in the yard. But plenty of prisoners like to read as well, often for practical reasons but also for entertainment or enlightenment.

Here are some of the most popular kinds of books in US prisons:

- Legal dictionaries
- GED Test prep guides
- *A Life Inside: A Prisoner's Notebook* by Erwin James
- *The 48 Laws of Power* by Robert Greene
- *The Bell Jar* by Sylvia Plath
- *The Diary of a Young Girl* by Anne Frank

THE BLIND ESCAPEE

Since the age of four, when he plotted to steal a neighbor's horse, Carl Synnerdahl had been running scams and cutting legal corners in Australia. He later graduated to theft and lucrative bank robberies, which funded a lavish lifestyle overseas. The only problem? He couldn't stop landing himself in prison.

After being extradited from Hong Kong, Synnerdahl was imprisoned again, this time for a six-year stint. Uninterested in serving out his term, but not wanting to attempt another brazen escape (he had tried that before and it ended up with a police chase and some shooting), he tried another angle.

Synnerdahl started acting as though he was losing his sight. He kept rubbing his eyes and bumping into things, using a cane and even learning Braille. The ruse worked, but only got him transferred to a lower-security prison. He finally escaped . . . only for police to catch him again within a week. They didn't take kindly to the cocky interviews he gave about conning them.

TRUE CRIME QUIZ

Which of these seemingly outdated charges was laid against Amanda Knox in an Italian court in 2011?

A. Witchcraft

B. Idolatry

C. Satanism

D. Having a child out of wedlock

Answer: A. A lawyer representing the man Knox claimed was responsible for the murder she was being charged with described her as an "enchanting witch."

THE TOOLBOX KILLERS

Part I: Things in Common

Lawrence Bittaker and Roy Norris first met in 1977 at the California Men's Colony prison in San Luis Obispo, California. Neither of them were pleasant characters, but they had certain similarities. Bittaker, whose adopted parents had disowned him after he committed too many crimes, had stabbed and nearly killed a supermarket worker a few years before. Norris, a foster kid who had been cut loose by the US Navy for his schizoid personality disorder, was a convicted rapist. Once the two got together, their collective evil intensified.

The pair came up with an insidious plan while on the inside. They decided that once on the outside, they would team up to kidnap, rape, and murder teenage girls. They planned to target one girl for each year (one for the age 13, 14, 15, and so on).

By January 1979, both had been released on parole. Bittaker bought a van, and after a few months, they were ready.

THE TOOLBOX KILLERS

Part II:

On June 24, 1979, Lawrence Bittaker and Roy Norris were driving their van along the Pacific Coast Highway when they spotted 16-year-old Cindy Schaefer. They stopped in front of her and dragged her into the van, bound, and gagged her. After driving into the woods, they strangled Schaefer and left her body.

Over the next five months, Bittaker and Norris kidnapped and killed five more girls between the ages of 13 and 18. In addition to raping some of their victims, they also tortured them. Later, they would be dubbed the "Toolbox Killers" because of the tools they used, which included pliers, knives, ice picks, and hammers.

Bittaker and Norris were such sadists that they also took pictures of their victims and recorded the sounds of their torture sessions.

The case broke when Norris bragged about his and Bittaker's crimes to a mutual friend, who told the police. After both were arrested in 1979, Norris turned on Bittaker to escape the death penalty. In 1981, Norris was sentenced to 45 years to life in prison, and Bittaker was sentenced to death. Eerily, they both died in prison of natural causes in 2019.

ORIGIN STORY
The Crips

Raymond Washington and Stanley "Tookie" Williams, students at Los Angeles's Washington High School, started their infamous gang, the Crips, around 1969. The boys adopted the school's color, blue, for the gang.

Multiple explanations have been given for the name: Some believe it is short for "cripple," a reference to the fact that some early members would use canes to disable their enemies.

Within a few years, the Crips had quickly grown in prominence and gained a reputation for violence. Gangs across the city started aligning with the Crips to gain protection and expand their reach. By the time Washington was murdered in a 1979 drive-by shooting, there were dozens of Crips satellite gangs across the city, often fighting with one another as much as with other gangs.

Saturday, July 18 2026

Sunday, July 19 2026

TERMINOLOGY

Filicide

As horrible as filicide (when a parent murders their child who is between the age of 1 and 18) is, it seems to have taken humanity a long time to deal with it. In ancient Greece and Rome, there were no laws to stop a father from killing his offspring. It was not until the 16th century that some European countries began to recognize filicide as a capital offense.

OAKLAND COUNTY CHILD KILLER

The first suspected victim of the so-called "Oakland County Child Killer" was Mark Stebbins. The 12-year-old from Ferndale, Michigan, called his mother on the afternoon of February 15, 1976, saying he was on his way home. His body was found in a parking lot snowbank four days later, with rope marks on his wrists and ankles. Stebbins had been sexually assaulted and strangled.

Over the next 13 months, the killer murdered three more children between the ages of 10 to 12. One was a boy, killed and abused in a similar way to Stebbins. The other two victims were girls, one smothered and the other killed by a shotgun, and neither sexually assaulted. When discovered, all four victims' bodies and clothes had been cleaned.

The investigation uncovered a child pornography ring operating from an island in Lake Michigan. But despite one of the largest manhunts in US history up to that time, the killer was never found.

DEPARTMENT OF IRONY

Convicted murderer Gary Gilmore, the subject of Norman Mailer's *The Executioner's Song*, was apparently a big fan of the Blue Öyster Cult song "Don't Fear the Reaper."

Another Gilmore note: British punk band the Adverts released their single "Gary Gilmore's Eyes" in 1977, the same year Gilmore was executed by firing squad. The tongue-in-cheek song imagines an eye transplant patient receiving the killer's eyes postexecution.

TRUE CRIME CLICHÉS

Have you heard this one before? Here are some of the most common tropes found in true crime podcasts, shows, or documentaries:

- “She could light up a room.”
- “It was a quiet town where people knew their neighbors and left their doors unlocked.”
- “He was known as a quiet man who kept to himself.”
- “They were high school sweethearts.”

See if you can come up with some of your own!

GUILT BY GOOGLE

Brian Walshe of Massachusetts was charged in 2023 with murdering his wife, Ana Walshe. Prosecutors listed some of the Google searches Walshe conducted before and after killing Walshe:

- "Hacksaw best tool to dismember"
- "How to clean blood from wooden floor"
- "How long before a body starts to smell"
- "Can you throw away body parts"

FEMALE SERIAL KILLERS ARE FROM VENUS

Part I

In a 2014 study from Penn State, researchers looked through every instance of a female serial killer they could find from 1821 to 2008. According to the findings summarized by lead author and psychology professor Marissa Harrison, the average female serial killer was:

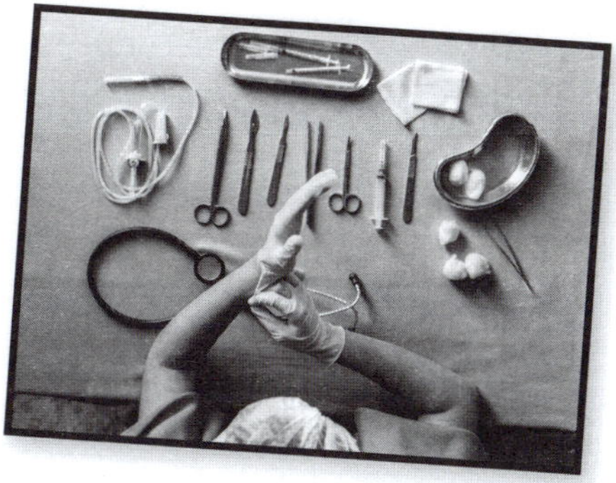

- White
- Educated
- Married at some point
- Christian
- Employed in a "caregiving" role (nearly 40 percent were healthcare workers or nurses)

Saturday, July 25 2026

Sunday, July 26 2026

FEMALE SERIAL KILLERS ARE FROM VENUS

Part II

Most male serial killers target people unknown to them. On the contrary, female serial killers are more likely to kill people they know—usually family members. Some other patterns in female serial killings, according to researcher Marissa Harrison, include:

- Most common weapon used: Poison
- Typical causes: Money or power
- They are often given girlish nicknames (e.g., Nannie Doss, the "Jolly Black Widow")

FEMALE SERIAL KILLERS ARE FROM VENUS

Part III

"Female serial killers exist. Usually movies, books, and podcasts focus on men. The FBI did not recognize female serial killers until the 1990s. . . . Women commit murder, and they get away with it."

—Marissa Harrison, *Just as Deadly*

CRIME DATA

A study by the UC Davis Violence Prevention Research Program published in the *Journal of Sports Economics* in May 2018 noted the remarkable effects televised sporting events have on criminal behavior in Chicago.

According to the study's authors, who pored over Chicago Police Department data from 2001 to 2013, crime in the city dropped by approximately 15 percent when the Chicago Bears were playing on *Monday Night Football*. Relatedly, crime dropped during the Super Bowl by roughly a quarter.

THE BOSTON STRANGLER

Part I: Panic City

On June 14, 1962, Boston police were called to the apartment of 55-year-old Anna Slesers. Her son had found her strangled to death, and the killer had left the belt of Slesers' torn-open housecoat tied around her neck in a bow. Slesers was the first victim of the killer who became known as the "Boston Strangler."

Over the next year and a half, 12 more women were killed in roughly the same manner in and around Boston. All the victims were single, and most lived alone. The attacks seemed to happen in the middle of the day and, in each case, the killer was apparently let in (no picked locks, broken windows, or kicked-in doors were found). Nobody heard any screams and there were no obvious signs of a struggle.

The panic that gripped Boston was palpable. Dead-bolt locks and door chains were sold out. Comparisons were made to Jack the Ripper. Police consulted a man who claimed the gift of "psychometry" to no avail.

The last of the Strangler's victims, 19-year-old Mary Sullivan, was raped and murdered in her apartment on January 4, 1964.

THE BOSTON STRANGLER

Part II: A Late Discovery

Albert DeSalvo spent much of his young life committing crimes. Among other things, he had a long record of sexual assaults. After one victim gave a description, DeSalvo was arrested and sent to Bridgewater State Hospital for a mental health evaluation. It was there in 1965 that one of the other residents, the convicted murderer George Nasser, said DeSalvo confessed to the Boston Strangler killings.

Despite DeSalvo confessing his guilt to Nasser and several other people, he was never charged with the murders and later retracted his confessions. Instead, in 1967 DeSalvo was sentenced to life in prison for earlier robbery and sexual assault charges. He was stabbed to death at Walpole State Prison in Massachusetts in 1973. None of the other suspects investigated by Boston police, including Nasser, were ever charged.

In 2013, DeSalvo's body was exhumed. DNA testing linked him to the Boston Strangler's last victim, Mary Sullivan.

Friday, July 31 2026

"This very hectic pace of life is one of the underlying causes of so many of our crimes. There are people who simply cannot adjust themselves to the new freedoms and the new stresses. They become misfits. Some of them are inept misfits; some are pathetic; some are dangerous misfits. Today we have the Mad Strangler of Boston. Yesterday we had the Mad Bomber in New York. Tomorrow we may have a Mad Murderer in your town or in mine."

—Erle Stanley Gardner, lawyer and author of the Perry Mason detective novel series

Saturday, August 1 2026

Sunday, August 2 2026

TRUE CRIME TRIVIA

Jeffrey Dahmer was known for cannibalizing some of the people he murdered. What characteristic would keep Dahmer from eating some of his other victims?

A. Long hair

B. Missing limb

C. Poor hygiene

D. Tattoos

Answer: D. He evidently believed that tattoo ink changed the taste of human flesh.

CRIME STATS

The US homicide clearance rate (the percentage of homicide cases considered closed by authorities) has been dropping for decades. Despite advanced technology, more murders in the US are going unsolved than ever before. Reasons are complex, but experts believe that low murder clearance rates impede future investigations and reinforce lack of trust in police. This dysfunction in turn makes people in areas with high gun violence less willing to cooperate with police investigations. The past 60 years, at a glance:

- 1965: 84 percent
- 1993: 63 percent
- 2022: 52 percent

CLOSE CALL
Catharine Lorre

Cousins Kenneth Bianchi and Angelo Buono were the serial killers known collectively as the Hillside Stranglers. When hunting for their prey in the Los Angeles area in the 1970s, they often pretended to be undercover police officers. They used this approach in November 1977 when they targeted Catharine Lorre.

Late one night as Catharine was walking home, Bianchi and Buono stopped her, showed their fake police badges, and asked for Lorre's identification. When they realized she was the daughter of actor Peter Lorre, whose work they were fans of (possibly including his representation of a serial killer in the noir film *M*), the two let her go on her way unharmed.

"One side of me says I'd like to talk to her, date her. The other side of me says, *I wonder what her head would look like on a stick?*"

—Ed Kemper, serial killer

RENT-A-HITMAN

When Josiah Ernesto Garcia was looking for money to help his family pay their rent, he came across an unusual website. Rentahitman.com offered the opportunity to apply for work as an assassin. Garcia applied, claiming he had been given the nickname "Reaper" for his sharpshooting skills while in the Tennessee Air National Guard.

After following up on his application multiple times, Garcia finally received a job offer. He met a man in a park, where he received photos and other information about his target, along with a down payment of $2,500. Then Garcia asked the man if he would require a picture of the dead body to prove the job was done.

Garcia was promptly arrested by his would-be employer, who turned out to be an undercover FBI agent. The website's founder, Bob Innes, said he intended it as a parody but kept getting inquiries from people who took it very seriously.

"I was looking into civilian law enforcement but that's not for me. I wanted something more exciting."

—Josiah Ernesto Garcia explaining to the FBI why he was interested in becoming an assassin for hire

Saturday, August 8 2026

Sunday, August 9 2026

THE MONSTER OF RILLINGTON PLACE

Part I: Lonely and Evil

In early 1953, Beresford Brown of 10 Rillington Place in London's then down-at-the-heels Notting Hill neighborhood was fixing up the kitchen in a recently vacated downstairs flat when he found a hidden compartment in the wall. Inside were the bodies of Hectorina MacLennan, Kathleen Maloney, and Rita Nelson. All three had been murdered by the previous tenant: John Christie.

The man later dubbed the "Monster of Rillington Place" grew up in Yorkshire as a lonely, disturbed young man fascinated by corpses and riddled with sexual hang-ups; rumors about his impotence led to nicknames like "Can't-Do-It-Christie." After serving in World War I, where he was hospitalized after a mustard gas attack, Christie embarked on a lifetime of intermittent employment, fractious married life, and petty crimes that soon spiraled into monstrous acts.

As with many other serial killers, Christie was obsessed with sex workers who would become his prey. In 1943, he committed his first known murder, strangling Ruth Fuerst to death during sex and burying her in the garden of his flat.

THE MONSTER OF RILLINGTON PLACE

Part II: An Unusual Method

John Christie had an unusual method of killing some of his victims. The second woman he killed, Muriel Eady, was invited in 1944 up to his flat, where he had convinced her he had a cure for her bronchitis. This "cure" turned out to be carbon monoxide gas. He raped and strangled the unconscious Eady, killing her and burying her body in the garden next to his first victim, Ruth Fuerst.

In 1948, married couple Timothy and Beryl Evans moved into the flat upstairs from Christie and his wife, Ethel. The next year, both Beryl and the Evans's baby, Geraldine, went missing. Timothy, a noted fabulist, kept changing his story and told the police several versions of what happened. In one version, he said that he (and later Christie) had tried to perform an abortion on the pregnant Beryl and accidentally killed her. Police found Beryl and Geraldine, both strangled to death and left in the building's outdoor washroom.

Based in part on Christie's testimony, Timothy was convicted and hanged in 1950. While the connection between Christie's murders and the killing of Beryl and Geraldine was not proven, it is assumed that Christie and Timothy Evans conspired together, given the statistical improbability of two murderers living so close to each other.

Tuesday, August 11 2026

THE MONSTER OF RILLINGTON PLACE

Part III: A Feverish Spree

The last phase of John Christie's killings started in 1952. Despite a period of keeping up appearances, Christie's ability to maintain a semblance of normalcy was deteriorating. He lost his job and sunk deeper into hypochondria. That December, his wife, Ethel, went missing. "She's gone back to her family in Sheffield," Christie told people. In reality, he had strangled her in bed with a stocking and buried her under the floorboards.

Christie killed his last three victims—Hectorina MacLennan, Kathleen Maloney, and Rita Nelson—in a feverish spree in early 1953. He gassed each into unconsciousness (using the same method of pretending carbon monoxide was a remedy), raped, and then strangled them to death, hiding them in the wall of his kitchen where they would be discovered after he moved out on March 20, 1953.

Days later, police arrested Christie, and he confessed to all the murders except that of the baby, Geraldine Evans. He was tried and put to death on July 15, 1953.

Timothy Evans was posthumously pardoned for his daughter's murder in 1996, and we may never know the true story.

"I remember as I gazed down at the still form of my first victim experiencing a strange, peaceful thrill. . . . It was thrilling because I had embarked on the career I had chosen for myself—the career of murder."

—John Christie, "The Monster of Rillington Place"

Thursday, August 13 2026

TERMINOLOGY

Behavioral analysis

When the Plainfield Police Department in New Jersey wanted help determining where crimes were most likely to happen, they turned to the private sector. In 2018, they started using the software PredPol, which promised to do just that. Not only did the software overwhelmingly predict more crimes in lower-income neighborhoods with more Black and Latino residents, but it was almost never correct. In one study of more than 23,000 crime predictions by the software, fewer than 100 matched a crime that actually occurred. So, not exactly *Minority Report*.

TRUE CRIME QUIZ

At its most powerful in the mid-1980s, the Medellin Cartel brought in roughly how much profit every day (largely cash) by smuggling cocaine?

A. $5 million

B. $20 million

C. $60 million

D. $100 million

Saturday, August 15 2026

Sunday, August 16 2026

Answer: C. $60 million.

"It became more of a problem to count the money and stack it. I mean, it took hours upon hours and hours to do it and recount it and go over and over it again. It was tedious as hell. Money became an obstacle. You know, it started to take the fun out of the whole thing, believe it or not."

—Cocaine trafficker George Jung on the challenges of managing his operation's massive profits

Monday, August 17 2026

TERMINOLOGY

Amber Alert

The child-abduction emergency response system was modeled after the warnings that are put out by the National Weather Service. The emergency notifications were created in response to the 1996 kidnapping of Amber Hagerman in Arlington, Texas, who was abducted just two blocks from her home and was found dead days later. The case remains open, and no suspects have ever been definitively identified. To prevent future tragedies like this, AMBER (America's Missing: Broadcast Emergency Response) alerts originally went out via radio and are now sent by text as soon as a child abduction is discovered and reported.

MIDTOWN JANE DOE

Part I: A Surprise

On February 10, 2003, construction workers preparing for the demolition of a building in Midtown Manhattan got a gruesome surprise. While they were knocking through a layer of somewhat fresh concrete in the basement, a human skull came rolling out.

They found a body in a fetal position wrapped in a carpet. An electrical cord was wrapped around her neck and binding her hands and feet. The remains appeared to be that of a young woman, likely 17 to 19 years old. There was no identification on her.

A few clues were found with the body:

- 1969 dime
- Ring with the initials "PMcG"
- 1960s Bulova watch
- Green plastic toy soldier

It was clear that she had gone missing in the late 1960s or early 1970s, but this was not enough for an identification.

She was named "Midtown Jane Doe" and the case went dormant.

MIDTOWN JANE DOE

Part II: A Name for the Dead

The case of Midtown Jane Doe was reopened by New York City detectives in 2017. This time, they had advanced forensic technology to help pull clues from her bones.

Although these early hopes went nowhere at first, six years later, in 2023, the detectives finally created a DNA profile for her. Using ancestry databases, they found a match for Doe's DNA somewhat by chance: A relative of the victim had given a DNA sample to New York's medical examiner after a family member died on 9/11. This finally gave them a name and identity, which they officially announced in April 2024.

Patricia Kathleen McGlone had been born in 1953. She was 16 years old, had given birth to a child, and had been living in Brooklyn's Sunset Park at the time of her death. Other than that, relatively little else is known about her life or who murdered her.

BLAMING THE VICTIM

During the 1960s, one of the glitziest nightspots in Glasgow, Scotland, was the Barrowland Ballroom. Three young women were murdered between 1968 and 1969 by somebody they had met at Barrowland. The killer, known as "Bible John" because a witness said the suspect had quoted scripture, was never caught.

In their notes, police described the dead using derogatory, misogynistic language. Unfortunately, such victim blaming is all too common in cases with female victims:

- "Rather spoiled"
- "Highly promiscuous"
- "Fond of male company"

Though the search for the killer was the largest ever carried out by Scottish police at the time, no arrests were made, and the murders remain unsolved.

"Tremble, thou wretch,
That hast within thee
undivulged crimes,
Unwhipp'd of justice."

—William Shakespeare, *King Lear*

Saturday, August 22 2026

Sunday, August 23 2026

CRIME STATS

A petty gangster who ran a pet shop and less legal affairs on the Lower East Side, Edward "Monk" Eastman was also a fixer and enforcer for New York's infamous Tammany Hall political machine. According to legend, Monk's thuggery-for-hire price list was very specific:

• Ear Chewed Off	$15.00
• Leg or Arm Broken	$19.00
• Shot in Leg	$25.00
• Stab	$25.00
• Doing the Big Job	$100.00 and up

STUDYING CRIME
Bryan Kohberger

The crime scene found at a nondescript rental home in Moscow, Idaho, on November 13, 2022, was among the most harrowing the town had ever seen. Bryan Kohberger, a 28-year-old criminology PhD student at nearby Washington State University, was accused of murdering four University of Idaho students there. They had all been stabbed to death with a long knife.

Kohberger, who was arrested in January 2023, had previously studied psychology and criminal justice at DeSales University in Pennsylvania. One of his teachers at DeSales was the forensic psychologist Katherine Ramsland, a renowned true crime author who has spent decades studying serial killers. Ramsland's books include *How to Catch a Killer* and *The Mind of a Murderer*.

TRUE CRIME QUIZ

What did Stephen Griffiths, who murdered several women in Bradford, England, during 2009 and 2010, call himself?

A. "Killer Diller"

B. "Crossbow Cannibal"

C. "Bradford Devil"

D. "Satan's Servant"

Answer: B. Griffiths killed at least two of his victims with a crossbow.

THE CRYPTO KILLING

Like many people, Lee Kyung-woo's business was hit hard during the COVID-19 pandemic. But he took an unusual route to get back on his feet, financially. After Lee's South Korea–based health club business failed, he put nearly all his money into a Seychelles-based cryptocurrency called Pure, only to see its value collapse in 2021.

That was when Lee created a new identity for himself. Claiming to be a former spy who had undertaken dangerous missions, he hired himself out to a couple who had also lost a fortune in Pure and were looking for revenge. The couple hired Lee to kidnap and murder a woman who had encouraged them to invest in the cryptocurrency.

In March 2023, the victim was snatched off a Seoul street and sedated with ketamine provided by Lee's wife, a nurse. The kidnappers let the woman regain consciousness long enough to try to coerce her into sharing the passwords necessary to steal her digital funds. When that failed, they gave her another, fatal, dose of ketamine and buried her body in the countryside.

Lee and his accomplices were all convicted. Pure was delisted in May, just a month after the victim was killed.

"I wanted to murder without casuistry, to murder for my own sake, for myself alone! I didn't want to lie about it even to myself."

—Rodion Raskolnikov in Fyodor Dostoyevsky's *Crime and Punishment*

Friday, August 28 2026

TIMOTHY KRAJCIR

Part I: Let Loose

First charged with petty crimes starting at the age of six in 1951, Timothy Krajcir later showed a penchant for stalking and sexual violence. He was first thrown into prison in 1963 for rape and attempted murder. Unfortunately, his worst crimes would follow his release in 1977. As part of his conditions of parole, he had to enroll in school. While studying for a degree in administrative justice at Southern Illinois University, Carbondale, he started his career as a serial killer.

Krajcir's first known victims were Mary Parsh and her daughter, Brenda Parsh. His pattern was to hunt for women who caught his eye. When one did, he would follow them and plan his attack once he determined they were not married or living with anybody else. He targeted Mary Parsh and was waiting at her house in nearby Cape Girardeau, Missouri, on the night of August 12, 1977, when she arrived home with Brenda. He raped Brenda and shot them both dead, then left to attend a friend's bachelor party.

Krajcir, who never seemed to understand the depth of what he did, served as a groomsman at his friend's wedding the next morning.

TIMOTHY KRAJCIR

Part II: Studying to Kill

Timothy Krajcir's crime spree ramped up after his murder of the Parshes in 1977. From that November to June 1982, he killed seven more women while still attending college and working as an ambulance driver. He proved difficult for police to pick up on, given the seemingly random and geographically dispersed nature of his attacks, along with the diverse ages and ethnicities of his victims and his varied weapons of choice. His understanding of police procedures, which he likely learned while studying for his administrative justice degree, led investigators to think the serial killer they were hunting was a fellow officer.

In 1982, the killing stopped when Krajcir returned to prison for a parole violation. Since then, various other charges (sexual assault of a minor, robbery, attempted escape) piled up and kept him behind bars and away from more potential victims.

In 2007, police were finally able to tie Krajcir to a murder through DNA testing. To avoid the death penalty, he took a plea deal, and pleaded guilty to the 1982 killing of Deborah Sheppard, a fellow student at Southern Illinois University, and five other women. He was given 13 consecutive life sentences.

"Seven out of ten times, when we hit a guy, we're wrong . . . but the other three times we hit, we make up for it."

—Mafia boss Sam "Momo" Giancana

Tuesday, September 1 2026

CRIME STATS

Popularity Contest

In a 2019 poll, US adults were asked which name came to mind first when thinking about serial killers:

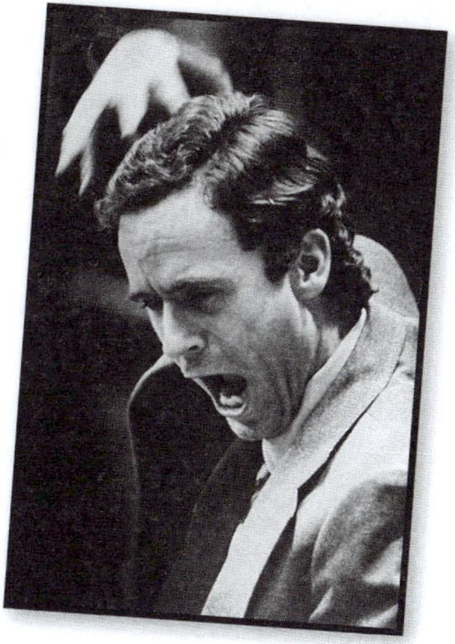

- 41 percent said Ted Bundy
- 21 percent said Jeffrey Dahmer
- 15 percent said Charles Manson
- 15 percent said John Wayne Gacy
- 6 percent* said Son of Sam

***When broken down by generation, the answers were still mostly the same for Generation X and Baby Boomers. However, Millennials did not answer "Son of Sam" in significant numbers; their fifth choice was "Zodiac Killer" at 2 percent.**

Wednesday, September 2 2026

EATING IN VEGAS

Early on the morning of April 28, 2024, Las Vegas police got a report about two men fighting near downtown. A 911 caller had reported one man attacking another. Arriving on the scene, they found one of the men fatally wounded and took the other into custody.

According to police, the attacker, Colin Ichiro Czech, had assaulted the victim and, during the course of the attack, eaten part of the man's face. Their report stated that Czech had "blood on his face and hands" along with "biological matter in his hair, mouth, and on his clothing."

Czech told police that he had been awake for five straight days because something was "possessing him" and that voices in his head told him to attack the victim, a stranger.

Thursday, September 3 2026

TERMINOLOGY

Odontology

This describes forensic usage of dentistry for identifying unknown people, whether possible suspects or the remains of the dead. It often involves using dental records (charts, X-rays) as well as the method of bite mark analysis, which was used to connect Ted Bundy to one of his victims, but has since been debunked for its lack of scientific validity.

TRUE CRIME QUIZ

Match the serial killer to the age they committed their first murder:

1.	James Fairweather	**A.**	12
2.	Harvey Miguel Robinson	**B.**	8
3.	Amarjeet Sada	**C.**	17
4.	Jasmine Richardson	**D.**	15

Answers: 1. D. At age 15, Fairweather stabbed his first victim more than 100 times. **2. C.** Robinson raped and murdered three women and then tried to kill the police as they tried to stop him from abducting a potential fourth victim. **3. B.** Sada's first murder was his baby cousin. **4. A.** Richardson killed her parents after they tried to stop her from dating a man twice her age.

“He is now in hell for eternity.”

—Justin Mohn, charged in January 2024 with homicide for allegedly decapitating his father with a machete and showing the head in a video he uploaded to YouTube. (Mohn called his father a “traitor” for being a veteran employee of the US federal government.)

THE RATCLIFFE HIGHWAY MURDERS

Part I: The Bloody Maul

The Ratcliffe Highway in London's East End might have been an ancient causeway dating back to antiquity, but by the early 19th century, it was little more than a nondescript thoroughfare through one of the city's less desirable neighborhoods on the Thames River. It was along this route in 1811 that a pair of brutal and inexplicable murders stunned the city.

On December 7, 1811, Margaret Jewell, house servant for the family of storeowner Timothy Marr, returned from an errand to 29 Ratcliffe Highway (the family's store and residence) to find the building dark and locked. After a while, a neighbor was able to get the door open. They found a horrible and blood-spattered scene: Timothy; his wife, Celia; their apprentice, James Gowan; and their three-month-old son were all dead.

Authorities had little to go on. The cash box was still full, suggesting robbery was not the motive. There were some bloody footprints and a carpenter's maul (likely the murder weapon) marked with the initials "J. P." Rewards were posted and many potential suspects were arrested, but no progress was made.

Then it happened again.

THE RATCLIFFE HIGHWAY MURDERS

Part II: Panic Spreads

Twelve days after the Marr family attack, the killer (or killers) struck again. This time, it was the household of another businessman. On the night of December 19, 1811, John Williamson; his wife, Elizabeth; and their servant, Bridget Anna Harrington, were all found murdered in the King's Arms, a tavern the Williamsons operated near the Ratcliffe Highway.

A watchman passing the tavern spotted one of its lodgers, John Turner, climbing down knotted bedsheets from a higher floor, in a state of undress, shouting, "Murder!" When the watchman entered the King's Arms, he found the Williamsons and Harrington with their throats slashed.

The neighborhood erupted in understandable panic, which quickly spread throughout London. Police searched houses and boats, stopping every wagon while fire bells rang out and volunteers were called to service. Newspapers demanded action, some claiming the murders were committed by a "foreign villain."

THE RATCLIFFE HIGHWAY MURDERS

Part III: Bring in the Usual Suspects

The Ratcliffe killings led to numerous arrests and accusations, but there was little evidence to go on. One man, a groom, was arrested because he had taken bloodstained clothes in for washing. A sailor, when questioned, claimed to know that seven killers had murdered the Marr family, but he later recanted, saying he had a fractured skull and didn't always know what he was saying.

The desperate desire to find a suspect finally landed on John Williams. Suspected of having an old grudge against Timothy Marr and living in the same inn where it was believed the Marr murder weapon (the bloodstained maul) had originated from, he was arrested.

On December 27, the magistrate summoned Williams, only to be told by a jailer that the suspected killer had been found dead from an apparent suicide. His body was displayed on a wagon and driven through the city. A stake was hammered through the heart of his corpse, and it was tossed into a hole in the ground. In 1887, workers digging a gas line discovered Williams's skeleton and took his skull.

For a short time, the skull decorated the bar at a nearby pub. Today, its whereabouts are unknown.

"For decades legends of the brutalities continued to circulate until, three-quarters of a century later, Jack the Ripper set to work on a neighboring East End stage to steal the limelight from his competitor for the sanguinary laurels of the British criminal calendar."

—P. D. James, *The Maul and the Pear Tree: The Ratcliffe Highway Murders 1811*

KILLER SONGS

It's hard to say what's older: our fascination with crime or our fascination with music. Murder ballads, a genre of folk songs that tell the story of a true crime or murder, have roots dating back to the Middle Ages. Traditionally, these songs often recounted sorrowful tales of husbands murdering their wives, but in more modern renditions, the tables are turned.

A few examples of modern murder ballads where the women do the murdering:

- "Goodbye Earl" by The Chicks
- "Two Black Cadillacs" by Carrie Underwood
- "The Night the Lights Went Out in Georgia" by Reba McEntire
- "no body no crime" by Taylor Swift
- "Man Down" by Rihanna

Saturday, September 12 2026

Sunday, September 13 2026

Grandparents Day (US)

"Murder will out."

—Geoffrey Chaucer, "The Nun's Priest's Tale," *The Canterbury Tales*

Monday, September 14 2026

THE TRIANGLE OF DEATH

Part I: The Missing

Between 1980 and 1987, several young men went missing in the Marne region in the northeast of France. After some bodies were discovered, the area gained a morbid nickname: the "Triangle of Death." Authorities were confounded by the cases and were unable to link them, even though several of the victims had been army conscripts, and they had all been last seen hitchhiking. The defense minister called the serial killer theory a "joke," while police dismissed worries of some of the disappeared men's mothers, who told them to stop "looking for a needle in a haystack."

Then in 1988, police stopped a van driven by Pierre Chanal, an instructor at the local Mourmelon army base and sergeant in the elite 4th Dragoons commando regiment. They were about to let him pass when someone began screaming, "Save me!" The cry came from Palazs Falvay, a Hungarian student and hitchhiker who Chanal had tied up in the back of the van. Convicted for kidnapping and raping Falvay, Chanal was imprisoned until 1995.

Then the investigation really began.

THE TRIANGLE OF DEATH

Part II : The Soldier

Pierre Chanal was often described as a model soldier with an excellent record, including decorations for service as a UN peacekeeper in Beirut during the Lebanese civil war. He had been serving as a military instructor at the same bases many of the alleged victims disappeared from.

Released from prison in 1995, Chanal was put under investigation for the murders of some of the young men whose bodies were discovered between 1980 and 1987. Their disappearances connected to times when he was in Mourmelon. Also, several pieces of evidence from Chanal's van—DNA from human hairs, a pair of underwear, and dirt on a shovel—connected him to three of the victims, including teenaged Irish tourist Trevor O'Keeffe.

After years of delay and what was described as a flagrantly mishandled investigation, Chanal finally went on trial for the three murders in 2003; five more murder charges could not be brought for lack of evidence. Chanal, who had gone on a hunger strike and threatened to kill himself, finally died by suicide in his cell: He slashed his wrists with a hidden razor blade just after the trial had begun. The French judicial system was ridiculed for its failure to give closure to any of the victims' families.

"If Patrice Denis, Patrick Gache, and Trevor [O'Keeffe] had been cabinet ministers' sons, there would have been a trial a long time ago."

—Eroline O'Keeffe, about the years of inattention paid to the kidnapping and murder of her son, Trevor O'Keeffe, and two other known victims of Pierre Chanal

ON THIS DAY

Patty Hearst, Urban Guerrilla

When the FBI arrested heiress Patty Hearst on September 18, 1975, she was just 21 years old. Despite her age, she had been one of the most widely hunted women in American history and, for a time, its most famous bank robber.

The granddaughter of immensely wealthy newspaper tycoon William Randolph Hearst, she was kidnapped from her Berkeley apartment on February 4, 1974, by the Symbionese Liberation Army (SLA), a leftist terrorist group. The SLA had already committed one murder and planned to use Hearst, the daughter of a pillar of the establishment they were fighting, for propaganda as a part of a larger revolutionary campaign.

A couple of months after being kidnapped, Hearst was seen on a security camera taking part in an SLA bank robbery. Dressed in a beret, she held a gun and called herself "Tania." Her whereabouts became a tabloid sensation. A shootout between authorities and the SLA in May ended in the deaths of six SLA members, but Hearst was nowhere to be found.

After Hearst was finally caught the following year, the public questioned whether she had been brainwashed or had willingly joined the SLA. She was given a seven-year prison sentence but served only two before it was commuted.

TERMINOLOGY

Malice aforethought

This term refers to a specific intent to kill or cause serious injury, where the person acted without regard for human life or engaged in a felony that led to a death. In some jurisdictions, proof of malice aforethought is required before a suspect can be charged with murder.

Saturday, September 19 2026

Sunday, September 20 2026 Yom Kippur begins at sundown

"My father was not the man I'd known him to be."

—Kerri Rawson, on discovering her father, Dennis Lynn Rader, was the BTK Killer

"I didn't want to hear that word, 'steal.' I kept saying, 'No, it's not stealing. I'm only taking what the man wants me to have.'"

—Doris Payne, renowned jewel thief who distracted clerks while trying on jewelry and walking out of the store with the goods

TRUE CRIME QUIZ

Which of these serial killers did *not* serve in the military?

A. Aileen Wuornos

B. Randy Kraft

C. Jeffrey Dahmer

D. David Berkowitz

Answer: A. Kraft joined the US Air Force in 1968 and was medically discharged on grounds of homosexuality the following year. Dahmer entered the US Army in 1979 and served as a combat medic in West Germany before being discharged in 1981 because of his drinking. Berkowitz served in the US Army from 1971 to 1974.

ART CRIME
Ana Mendieta

One of the many unaccompanied minors sent from Cuba to the US during the Cuban Revolution as part of Operation Peter Pan, Ana Mendieta came to the country in 1961 when she was 12 years old. While at the University of Iowa, she made provocative art about sexual violence against women and, after she relocated to New York City in 1978, she quickly gained a name in the art world.

Mendieta met the famed minimalist sculptor Carl Andre in 1979. Their relationship was described as combative, with heavy drinking exacerbating their arguments. After the two married on January 16, 1985, things seemed to stabilize for a while. But conflict soon reared up again.

Late on September 8, 1985, Mendieta fell to her death from the 34th-story window of their Mercer Street apartment in Greenwich Village—it is not clear whether she jumped, fell, or was pushed. After some delay, Andre was charged with her murder. A doorman claimed to have heard someone shout, "No, no, no" before Mendieta hit the pavement. Andre's defense said she had died by suicide.

Andre was acquitted and carried on with his career, though many in the art world continued to have suspicions.

Today, Mendieta is remembered as a pioneering feminist artist.

"What happened was we had . . . my wife is an artist and I am an artist and we had a quarrel about the fact that I was more, eh, exposed to the public than she was and she went to the bedroom and I went after her and she went out of the window."

—Carl Andre's 911 call on September 8, 1985

TRUE CRIME QUIZ

Connect these rock stars with the criminal charge that put them behind bars (even if just briefly):

1. Paul McCartney
2. Keith Moon
3. Keith Richards
4. Johnny Rotten

A. Striking an officer

B. Half pound of marijuana found in luggage

C. Knocking over a computer, riding a wheelchair down a staircase, and waving a fake gun in an airport

D. Amphetamines found in home

Saturday, September 26 2026

Sunday, September 27 2026

Answers: 1. B. 2. C. 3. D. 4. A. (per Rotten, aka Lydon, he was "arrested for attacking a policeman's fist with my face").

"I wish you all had one neck and that I had my hands on it."

—Carl Panzram, executed in 1930 for multiple murders

Monday, September 28 2026

EXONERATED

David Milgaard

On January 31, 1969, 16-year-old Winnipeg native David Milgaard had just arrived in Saskatoon, Saskatchewan, Canada, with a couple of friends. They crashed at the house of another friend, Albert Cadrain, before the four took off together on a road trip to Calgary.

After returning from the trip a few weeks later, Cadrain contacted police. He told them that when Milgaard showed up on January 31, his clothes were bloodstained and he seemed to be in a rush. Police were looking for a suspect in the killing of Gail Miller, a nursing student who had been raped and stabbed to death in an alley near Cadrain's home around the time Milgaard and his friends had arrived in town.

Despite Cadrain changing his story and a lack of evidence against Milgaard, the latter was arrested for murder on May 30, 1969, and after a trial was given a life sentence. During his imprisonment, Milgaard suffered abuse, and he tried to kill himself multiple times. He briefly escaped in 1980, but was soon recaptured.

Milgaard's mother fought to clear his name. Through her own investigation, she found another suspect, Larry Fisher, whose ex-wife had reported him to police as a suspect in Miller's murder in 1980. Milgaard was finally freed in 1992 and his innocence was officially confirmed in 2004, following DNA testing.

TERMINOLOGY

Identi-Kit

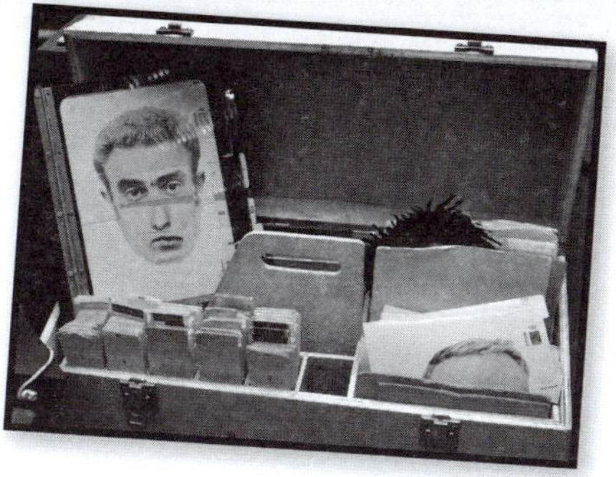

First introduced in the 1950s by Los Angeles detective Hugh C. McDonald, Identi-Kits were originally sets of materials (hair, glasses, lips, noses, eyes) that officers could assemble based on eyewitness descriptions to create a likeness of a suspect. Today, these have been replaced by computer software.

WHAT HAPPENED TO SHANQUELLA ROBINSON?

In October 2022, North Carolina businesswoman Shanquella Robinson took a vacation with six friends to a resort in San José del Cabo, Mexico. The trip took a dark turn on October 29, when a doctor was called to the resort to check on Robinson. Her friends, who seemed reluctant to have her admitted to the hospital, said that she had alcohol poisoning. Robinson went into cardiac arrest and died later that day.

Suspicions about the case began to mount. An autopsy found her cause of death to be "severe spinal cord injury" from wounds on her neck and spine. Some of Robinson's travel companions gave inconsistent accounts of what had happened.

Then a viral video began to circulate that suggested there was something more intentional about Robinson's death. In the video, another woman severely beat Robinson as the man recording the video can be heard saying, "Quella, can you at least fight back?"

Despite the work of Robinson's family and Mexican journalists to uncover more about the story, US authorities declined to press charges.

"Six witnesses . . . are alive and haven't fled anywhere. They have the same cell phone numbers that they had when the crime transpired. If the FBI can open up files on Malcolm X and Martin Luther King for no reason, why can't they [investigate] six people who [may be] involved in the murder of a US citizen on video?"

—Sue-Ann Robinson, lawyer to Shanquella Robinson's family (no relation)

TRUE CRIME QUIZ

In *Dirty Harry* (1971), Clint Eastwood's San Francisco detective Harry Callahan hunts a serial killer terrorizing the city with seemingly random sniping attacks. Which real-life killer was the movie's inspiration?

A. Charles Manson

B. Zodiac Killer

C. Richard Speck

D. The Torso Killer

Saturday, October 3 2026

Sunday, October 4 2026

Answer: B. The killer in *Dirty Harry* liked to send mocking, cryptic letters to the press that taunted police and gave himself an astrological nickname, "Scorpio," just like the Zodiac Killer. A San Francisco detective who inspired Eastwood's character reportedly walked out of a screening of *Dirty Harry* because it so closely resembled the then-still-ongoing Zodiac investigation.

CRIME DATA

CSI *Effect*

Not long after the *CSI* crime drama series started in 2000, law enforcement authorities began to be concerned about what they call the "*CSI* Effect." This is the belief that juries, who may have seen the show's heroes solve crimes using high-tech forensic analysis, may be less likely to convict without forensic evidence, which is far less commonly available in real-world criminal cases than it is on *CSI*.

There is not much hard data to suggest this prejudice can be linked to a popular TV series. Nevertheless, a National Institute of Justice study found that potential jurors have unrealistic expectations for evidence:

- Expecting to see scientific evidence in every criminal case: 46 percent
- Expecting to see fingerprint evidence: 36 percent
- Expecting to see ballistic or other firearms evidence: 32 percent
- Expecting to see DNA evidence: 22 percent

"If once a man indulges himself in murder, very soon he comes to think little of robbing; and from robbing he comes next to drinking and sabbath-breaking, and from that to incivility and procrastination."

—Thomas De Quincey, 19th-century essayist and literary critic

COPS GONE BAD

Some officers of the law have used their positions and training not to catch killers but to hide their own ugly murderous habits:

- Norbert Poehlke: A veteran police inspector in Stuttgart, Germany, he was implicated in three murders from 1984 to 1985. In each case, Poehlke would rob a bank, kidnap a driver for his getaway, and then murder the driver. He died by suicide in 1985 after his fellow officers got wise to him.
- Mikhail Popkov: Over at least two decades, Russian policeman Mikhail Popkov killed dozens of women while on duty, largely in the remote Irkutsk region, before he was captured. In 2023, he tried to shorten his sentence by volunteering to fight for Russia in their war against Ukraine.
- Gerard Schaefer: During his time as a South Florida police officer, Schaefer kidnapped, raped, and hanged numerous young women to death before he was captured and sent to prison.

TERMINOLOGY

Latent print

A latent print is a fingerprint left on a surface (resulting from accumulated oils and sweat on the skin that leave patterns behind) and not immediately visible. Investigators, who use a fingerprint powder (talcum for lighter surfaces, graphite for darker) to see where latents have been left, may use these prints to connect suspects with being present at a crime scene.

"Police officers a hundred years ago were often not respected by juries because, in truth, they very often were not worthy of much respect. They are better educated now; they have better uniforms and better PR guys. This probably causes juries to give them more credence. This is perhaps unfortunate. Professionals lie just as often as amateurs, only more skillfully."

—Bill James, *Popular Crime: Reflections on the Celebration of Violence*

CARIBBEAN PIRACY

The Case of Simplicity

On February 21, 2024, the catamaran *Simplicity* was discovered in Saint Vincent and the Grenadines without any crew. The boat was owned by an American couple, Kathy Brandel and Ralph Hendry, who had recently left Hampton, Virginia, to sail around the Caribbean on their way to Aruba. Although the couple was nowhere to be found, the boat was described as "ransacked" and there were signs that a fight had occurred.

Several days later, the Royal Grenada police provided a clue to the mystery: Three men had escaped prison in Grenada on February 18, and, like modern-day pirates, had hijacked and commandeered Brandel and Hendry's boat. The police said the suspects had likely "committed several criminal acts including bodily harm to the couple."

The three men were charged that March with capital murder and multiple other offenses. At the time, Brandel's and Hendry's bodies had not been discovered, and they were presumed dead.

Saturday, October 10 2026

Sunday, October 11 2026

THE GOLDEN DRAGON MASSACRE

In the 1960s and 1970s, strife between Chinese American street gangs in San Francisco began to escalate, in part because of the arrival of newer Chinese immigrants with more violent backgrounds. One of the larger beefs was between the Joe Boys and the Wah Ching gangs, who were fighting for control of the city's Chinatown.

The gang war came to a head on Saturday, September 3, 1977. Late that night, several teenage members of the Joe Boys found out some Wah Ching members were hanging out at the Golden Dragon restaurant in Chinatown. Looking for revenge following a shoot-out a couple months before, the Joe Boys stormed into the Golden Dragon, opening fire with shotguns and an assault rifle. The deadly barrage of bullets killed 5 people and left another 11 wounded. The assassins had been aiming for rival gangsters, but they ended up killing only civilians, including a waiter and a tourist.

Though the war had been percolating for some time, the Golden Dragon Massacre pushed the city's authorities to act. A gang task force was set up by law enforcement and the Joe Boys dissolved following the convictions of several of the shooters in the massacre.

"I think crime pays. The hours are good, you travel a lot."

—Woody Allen, *Take the Money and Run* (1969)

TERMINOLOGY

Chain of custody

This is the process by which law enforcement documents the collection, identification, transfer, and storage of evidence relating to a crime. If the chain of custody is not appropriately followed (e.g., mishandling of evidence), it is referred to as "broken" and that error can be used as part of an argument for the evidence to be ruled as inadmissible.

CATCHING JOUBERT

Part I: Deadly But Social

In some ways, John Joubert did not fit the profile of a potential serial killer. Though bullied and teased growing up in Portland, Maine, Joubert was an honor roll student, a school athlete, and a Boy Scout. From an early age, however, he had myriad ugly fantasies ranging from strangling (he had witnessed his father choking his mother, whom he hated) or stabbing tied-up victims to cannibalization.

In December 1979 at the age of 16, Joubert came up behind a 6-year-old girl on his bicycle while riding his newspaper delivery route and stabbed her nonfatally with a pencil. Several weeks later, Joubert grabbed a college student from behind and stabbed her with a knife, again nonfatally.

Following other unprompted assaults, Joubert graduated from high school and briefly attended college. Then, in August 1982, the body of 11-year-old Richard Stetson was found near a jogging trail in Portland. He had been stabbed, strangled, and bitten. Not long after, Joubert left Maine for Nebraska, where he started a tour of duty in the Air Force and would soon find new victims.

CATCHING JOUBERT

Part II: Hunting

In 1983, John Joubert was far from the scene of his crimes in Portland, Maine. He served as a radar technician at the Air Force base in Offutt, Nebraska. But his violent fantasies continued.

Late that September, 13-year-old Danny Joe Eberle went missing while on his morning paper delivery route. He was discovered days later in the woods near Bellevue, Nebraska, dead from multiple stab wounds. His hands and ankles were tied by rope, and there were several bite marks on his body.

A second murder followed in December. Twelve-year-old Christopher Paul Walden was kidnapped on his way to school. His body was also found several days later, with similar stab wounds and mutilations.

By this point, local residents were terrified. But the police were on the case, and the FBI soon joined the manhunt as well.

CATCHING JOUBERT

Part III: The Feds Arrive

The FBI became involved in the hunt for the killer of two young boys in the Omaha, Nebraska, suburb of Bellevue because they had also been kidnapped, which elevated the case to the federal level. The agency's still-developing Behavioral Science Unit tried to create a profile of the likely killer through the work of pioneering criminal personality researcher Ann Burgess.

Joubert was caught in January 1984 after a preschool teacher noticed him suspiciously driving around near the school. Further investigation and FBI profiling connected Joubert to the attacks back in Maine. When caught, he confessed to killing the two boys in Nebraska.

Found guilty of all three murders, Joubert spent several years on death row. He was executed in the electric chair on July 17, 1996.

Saturday, October 17 2026

Sunday, October 18 2026

"I didn't know 'em, how could I dislike 'em?"

—John Joubert, when asked whether he had any bad feelings toward the boys he murdered

HEISTS

Pierre Hotel

One of the largest armed robberies in US history did not involve a bank or armored car. Instead, it took place at one of the world's most luxurious hotels.

Robert Comfort and Sammy Nalo were skilled high-end thieves. In 1971, they had snatched $1 million in cash and jewels from legendary film star Sophia Loren's suite at Manhattan's famed Sherry Netherland hotel. The men put together another heist targeting the similarly high-end Pierre hotel on Central Park East. This time, they brought in extra muscle from the Lucchese crime family and various other crooks, including famed jewel thief Nick "The Cat" Sacco.

The heist was planned for January 2, 1972, based on the assumption (which turned out to be correct) that security would be light and the safe deposit boxes loaded. The eight-man team took over the lobby around 3:00 a.m., emptying deposit boxes and tying up the staff and guests who were present.

The team got away with about $3 million (though it has been suggested the take was actually $28 million, which Comfort and Nalo kept secret from their confederates), giving each of their hostages $20 on their way out.

TRUE CRIME QUIZ

Connect these nicknames to their gangster:

1. Tick-Tock	**A.** Philip Testa
2. The Nose	**B.** Michael Mancuso
3. Chicken Man	**C.** Gerlando Sciascia
4. George from Canada	**D.** Albert Tannenbaum

Answers: 1. D. This Murder, Inc., assassin gained his moniker because his constant chattering was like a clock. **2. B.** Despite his unthreatening nickname, Mancusco was a Bonanno family underboss in the 2000s. **3. A.** Testa, who was once in the poultry business, was killed by a nail bomb, which is how he gets referenced in the opening line of Bruce Springsteen's "Atlantic City." **4. C.** After emigrating from Sicily, Sciascia moved first to Montreal, Canada (the Mafia never insisted on originality in nicknames).

TERMINOLOGY

Involuntary manslaughter

This term refers to an act that unintentionally leads to another person's death. In one example, the actor Alec Baldwin and film armorer Hannah Gutierrez-Reed were charged with involuntary manslaughter after the accidental discharge of a pistol on a film set in 2021 caused the death of cinematographer Halyna Hutchins.

THE END OF FABIO

Beauty salon industry executive Fabio Sementelli was at his Los Angeles, California, home on January 23, 2017, when he was stabbed to death by two intruders. At first, authorities believed the assault was a robbery gone bad; however, investigators discovered blood at the scene that was not Fabio's, which, on its own, was not enough to arouse suspicion. But then they found out his wife, Monica Sementelli, had been having an affair with racquetball coach Robert Baker.

When authorities found blood from Baker inside Fabio's Porsche, which was seen on a security camera being driven away from the house at the time of the murder and later abandoned, they began to focus on Monica and Baker as suspects in Fabio's killing.

After the pair was caught and arrested, Monica was recorded saying to Baker, "Somebody must have talked." The two were indicted for murder and conspiracy. Baker was later sentenced to life in prison, but insisted Monica had nothing to do with the killing. In October 2024, a third suspect, Christopher Austin, was charged. He said that the three of them conspired to kill Fabio for his insurance money, undermining Monica's claim of innocence.

ON THIS DAY

Albert Anastasia

By the 1950s, Albert Anastasia was one of the American Mafia's living legends. One of the cofounders of Murder, Inc., he was born in Italy in 1902 and came to America as a teenager. Eking out a tough living as a longshoreman in New York, he was imprisoned for his first murder in 1921. Ten years later, Anastasia helped bring about the assassination of his onetime Mafia boss Joe Masseria. Anastasia kept climbing the ranks of organized crime as his rivals and various witnesses to his crimes met unfortunate ends.

Anastasia had built himself a fortresslike house on the high Hudson River cliffs in Fort Lee, New Jersey. Despite that, he kept some old habits that didn't lend well to security, even as enemies plotted his downfall.

On October 25, 1957, Anastasia had his driver take him into Manhattan for an appointment with his barber at the Park Sheraton. When Anastasia's bodyguard stepped away, a pair of masked killers charged in, unleashing a fusillade of gunfire that ended the intrepid old mobster.

Saturday, October 24 2026

Sunday, October 25 2026

"There are four kinds of homicide: felonious, excusable, justifiable, and praiseworthy, but it makes no great difference to the person slain whether he fell by one kind or another—the classification is for advantage of the lawyers."

—Ambrose Bierce, 19th-century journalist and author

THE CASE OF THE SELFIE KILLER

Amanda Taylor had been deeply in love with her husband, Rex. The two Virginians shared a fascination with violence, murder, and serial killers, and Amanda even fantasized about becoming one herself. But their dark romance took an even darker turn after Rex hanged himself in August 2014.

Amanda became convinced that Rex's father, 59-year-old Charles Taylor, was responsible for giving his son the opioids that caused his addiction and may have led to his suicide. This rage, combined with Amanda's morbid fantasies, may have pushed her toward making them a reality.

Amanda and her friend Sean Bell broke into her father-in-law's house in 2015. Bell hit Charles in the head with a tire iron while Amanda stabbed him dozens of times.

Amanda took a picture of Charles's body and herself holding a bloody knife, which she posted on social media. Then she and Bell went on the run. Amanda tried to talk Bell into going on a killing spree with her but, when he refused, she shot him in the face, nonfatally. Leaving him for dead, she took a picture of his body before she drove away. Amanda would soon earn infamy as the "Selfie Killer." She was caught and arrested soon after, and is serving a life sentence.

"I was just really excited and I was like, 'Hey, I'm gonna take a picture so I can post it and show everyone.' . . . It made me really happy."

—Amanda Taylor, the "Selfie Killer"

ONE LAST VICTIM

The night of March 18, 1978, was not the first time that Myrtie and her husband Bill Moon's small South Carolina grocery had been robbed, but it would be the last. Rudolph Tyner, an 18-year-old from New York City, demanded Bill give him all the money he had. When Bill said no, Tyner shot him and then Myrtie dead, taking $200 from the register and fleeing.

After multiple trials, Tyner was convicted of murder and given the death penalty. But he did not live long enough to be executed. Myrtie's son and Bill's stepson, Tony Cimo, had vowed revenge. He got in touch with Donald "Pee Wee" Gaskins, a serial killer serving multiple consecutive life sentences in the same prison with Tyner, who happily agreed to Cimo's cash offer.

A cellblock maintenance chief who seemed to have unusual freedom for an imprisoned murderer, Gaskins was eventually able to get the materials necessary for the job. He rigged a radio with explosives, convinced Tyner to listen, and plugged it in; the resulting explosion killed Tyner and nearly vaporized his head. Gaskins was later executed in 1991. Cimo was convicted of conspiracy to commit murder and sentenced to 8 years in prison.

"I just got hysterical strength."

—Jennifer Asbenson, a 19-year-old hitchhiker who, after being tied up and put in the trunk of a car in 1992 by murderer Andrew Urdiales, broke free and escaped

Friday, October 30 2026

TERMINOLOGY

Social cleansing

This is a term used in some South American countries (translated from "limpieza social") to describe the generally wanton murder of people seen as having lower socioeconomic status. From the late 1980s to early 1990s, hundreds of "undesirables" (e.g., unhoused people, petty criminals) were estimated to have been killed by vigilantes. In one 1993 case, Brazilian police were found to have executed eight unhoused youths in front of a church in Rio de Janeiro.

THE SNOWTOWN MURDERS

Part I: Gathering a Crew

The most infamous serial killings ever to occur in Australia started with one man and some notes on a wall. John Justin Bunting, a maladjusted man from Adelaide, South Australia, was obsessed with people he considered to be gay or pedophiles (he seemed to blur the two very different categories). A one-time slaughterhouse worker, he was fascinated by weaponry, and Bunting created what he called a "rock spider wall" ("rock spider" being slang for pedophile), where he put up pictures and information about the various people he was targeting.

Seemingly less of a loner than many serial killers, Bunting put together a group of confederates who could help with his plans. With the assistance of some friends and family (including his wife, Elizabeth Harvey, and her son, James Vlassakis), he began carrying out his attacks.

Bunting lured Clinton Trezise, a 22-year-old man Bunting believed to be a pedophile, into his home and beat him to death with a shovel. Three years later, Bunting, Harvey, and a friend stabbed and strangled to death Ray Allan Peter Davies, who had been in a relationship with Bunting's ex-girlfriend.

Monday, November 2 2026

THE SNOWTOWN MURDERS

Part II: Disposing of Remains

Having recruited three others into his ad hoc Australian murder squad, John Justin Bunting spent a good part of the 1990s putting them to work. In addition to the men he targeted for supposedly being gay or sexual predators, Bunting also seemed to choose male and female victims for no apparent reason. One commonality, however, was his desire to extract misery and money from each of them.

Many of the dozen victims Bunting and his gang killed were tortured fiendishly. The infliction of pain was not the only goal for the sadistic and power-obsessed Bunting, but a means to a dark end. Bunting and his gang robbed their victims and also extracted information from them, which they then used to steal bank balances and welfare payments.

Their scheme was discovered on May 20, 1999. Police, searching for Elizabeth Haydon (the wife of Bunting's accomplice, Mark Haydon, who the gang had killed the previous November) found the remains of eight people dissolved in multiple barrels of acid hidden in an old bank in Snowtown, a small village north of Adelaide.

THE SNOWTOWN MURDERS

Part III: The Bank Building

John Justin Bunting's murder crew were connected to a dozen killings in the so-called "bodies in barrels" case. Most of their victims had been disposed of in that way. Two more bodies were dug up in the yard of a former residence of Bunting's. One victim, Thomas Eugenio Trevilyan—a mentally ill man who had helped Bunting kill another of his victims—had not been disposed of, but was killed by being hanged from a tree. When his body was discovered in November 1997, the death was written off as a suicide. The last of Bunting's victims was David Johnson, stepbrother to Bunting's accomplice, James Vlassakis. After torturing Johnson to death in the Snowtown bank building, the attackers cooked and ate part of his body.

Bunting himself received 11 consecutive life terms. The nearly yearlong trial was so harrowingly detailed, some jury members had to receive therapy.

"Driving back from Snowtown that first day, through the urban wasteland of the welfare-dependent northern suburbs, I wondered: have we grown an under class, born out of boredom and poverty and disaffection, that is becoming increasingly warped, increasingly violent and from whom we must turn away lest they catch our eye? Have we created a Gothic underworld of marginalised people?"

—Debi Marshall, *Killing for Pleasure: The Definitive Story of the Snowtown Serial Murders*

Thursday, November 5 2026

TRUE CRIME TRAVEL

These are some of the top US cities to visit for true crime buffs, with a plethora of tours of famous crime sites:

- New Orleans
- New York City
- Chicago
- Seattle
- Washington, DC

"SOMEONE IS GOING TO DIE"

The 2015 marriage of Keir and Grace Johnston became internet famous because of what started as a mild disagreement over a dress. One of their wedding guests shared a picture on social media of the dress worn by Grace's mother and asked people to help resolve a dispute: Was the dress black and blue, or white and gold? (The answer is clearly black and blue, but some saw otherwise.) The viral debate that ricocheted around the world became known as "the dress that broke the internet."

After their moment of fame, Keir and Grace moved to the isle of Colonsay off the west coast of Scotland. The next time they appeared in the news, it was for more serious reasons than the color of a dress. Grace alleged that she began to be afraid for her life after Keir started threatening her. There were no police on their lonely island, and Grace felt trapped. She later revealed that in March 2022, Keir began strangling her and told her "someone is going to die."

Keir pleaded guilty to endangering Grace's life in May 2024.

Saturday, November 7 2026

Sunday, November 8 2026

Diwali begins

TRUE CRIME QUIZ

Which of the following reputed mobsters once ran Los Angeles's "Six Families"?

A. John Gotti

B. Jackie "The Nose" D'Amico

C. "Handsome Johnny" Roselli

D. Meyer Lansky

E. None of the above

Answer: E. None of them. Gotti and D'Amico operated out of New York, Roselli in Chicago, and Lansky originally in New York but later worked in Miami. Also, the Los Angeles mob was less organized than those back East; there were only five (not six) "families" in the Mafia's brief attempt at organization; and the syndicate was in New York, not Los Angeles.

HEISTS
The Kardashian Jewels

On October 2, 2016, billionaire reality TV star Kim Kardashian and some of her family were attending Paris Fashion Week. They did not know they were being targeted by a jewelry theft gang. That night, five men entered the lobby of the popular guesthouse where Kardashian was staying. They handcuffed the concierge and forced him at gunpoint to open the door to Kardashian's penthouse suite.

The robbers found Kardashian alone; her bodyguard had accompanied her sister and half sister to a nightclub. Initially angered that she had little cash on her, the robbers taped her mouth shut to stop her terrified screaming. The crew's initial idea was to hit every room in the guesthouse. But once Kardashian's bodyguard started calling her phone, the robbers decided to get out, fleeing into the night on their bicycles.

They did well for a short night's work, netting roughly $5.6 million worth of jewelry and other items (including a $4 million 20-carat diamond ring bought by Kanye West) in less than an hour. The robbers were caught and arrested three months after the heist.

FATHER JUAN SEVERINO MALLARI

Part I: A Priest of the People

Parishioners of San Bartolome Church in the Philippines region of Magalang, which sits about 60-odd miles northwest of Manila, were excited for the arrival in 1816 of their new parish priest, Father Juan Severino Mallari. As a native Filipino, Mallari was a welcome change from the Anglo priests who usually filled such roles. He was a talented calligrapher and was widely trusted by his flock.

That happiness, however, soon turned to horror. Corpses of disappeared people began showing up in the area. At some point after arriving at San Bartolome, Mallari's mother had become sick, and he was spiraling. His Catholic faith did not keep him from thinking that his mother had somehow been cursed by a "mangkukulam," or witch. Mallari's confused mind convinced him that the only way to save his mother was to start killing his parishioners.

According to Mallari's way of thinking, he was performing a kind of sacrifice, and the more parishioners he killed, the greater chance of his mother's survival.

It's time! Order your 2027 *True Crime Calendar.*

Visit **pageaday.com** to browse all of our fun and inspiring calendars. If you like this calendar, you may find these just your style, too:

With Workman Calendars, **don't just count the days; make the days count.** A calendar can indulge your passion every day of the year—whether it provides a laugh, a brain challenge, a bit of inspiration, or something new to learn. And calendars make great gifts!

Sign up for our newsletter at **pageaday.com/news** to receive information about new books and calendars, our cat and dog photo contests, special promotions, and more!

Order next year's calendar at **pageaday.com**

FATHER JUAN SEVERINO MALLARI

Part II: Last Rites

Father Juan Severino Mallari's murder spree began around 1816. For years afterward, bodies were found all over the Magalang region. There was little by way of clues, motives, or similarities among them to tie the victims together. This added another challenge on top of the era's early criminology.

For years, the killings continued, despite what seemed to be Mallari's increasingly psychotic behavior. Then, in 1826, Mallari fell physically sick. When a different priest came to check on Mallari, he discovered something besides an ill pastor. Mallari's chambers contained numerous personal items of the victims, some apparently covered in blood.

Suspected of killing a staggering 57 people to break the witch's curse he believed was afflicting his mother, Mallari was put on trial for murder. This was done despite the pleas of a doctor to put Mallari in a mental hospital. Mallari was found guilty, imprisoned, and then executed by hanging in 1840. He gained the unfortunate distinction of being the Philippines' first known serial killer.

WHERE DO SERIAL KILLERS COME FROM?

The recipe for creating a serial killer is still largely mysterious, falling as it does into familiar nature versus nurture debates. However, data does exist to show what *places* are more likely to create or at least be inhabited by serial killers. Here are the US states with the highest number of serial murders per 1 million inhabitants:

- Alaska: 15.65
- Nevada: 12.19
- Florida: 9.92
- California: 7.81
- Washington: 7.44

Friday, November 13 2026

A CATFISH MURDER IN ALASKA

The man who called himself Tyler said a lot of things online. He described himself as a millionaire from Indiana, used fake pictures, and claimed that he would pay somebody $9 million if they could send him a video of a real murder. In reality, Tyler was 21-year-old Indiana native Darin Schilmiller, and he was nothing close to being a millionaire. Some people, however, became besotted enough by his fakery that they did what "Tyler" asked.

In 2019, Anchorage, Alaska, teenager Denali Brehmer took Schilmiller up on his offer. She convinced several other teenagers to join her scheme; they lured Cynthia Hoffman to go on a hike. Hoffman, a vulnerable 19-year-old with developmental disabilities, believed these people were her friends and went along. In an isolated area, the attackers tied Hoffman with duct tape, shot her in the back of the head, and disposed of her body in the Eklutna River. After Brehmer sent photos and videos of the murder to Schilmiller, he revealed that he never had the money he promised her.

Both Schilmiller and Brehmer were convicted of Hoffman's murder. They each received 99-year sentences.

Saturday, November 14 2026

Sunday, November 15 2026

"Dead people belong to the live people who claim them most obsessively."

—James Ellroy, *My Dark Places: An L.A. Crime Memoir*

Monday, November 16 2026

TRUE CRIME QUIZ

Match the book with the name of the criminal(s) it was about:

1. *The Orchid Thief* by Susan Orlean
2. *Killers of the Flower Moon* by David Grann
3. *Midnight in the Garden of Good and Evil* by John Berendt
4. *The Stranger Beside Me* by Ann Rule

A. Ted Bundy

B. John Laroche

C. William King Hale

D. Jim Williams

Answers: 1. B. Orlean's acclaimed book was an unusually murder-free true crime book about a poacher of rare orchids. **2. C.** Hale comes across in Grann's book about the 1920s Osage Country murder spree as one of the lesser-known diabolical mass murderers in American history. **3. D.** Berendt's massively popular bestseller was just as much about a complex murder mystery as the Savannah culture where it happened. **4. A.** Rule's book about serial killer Bundy was her first and based in part on her having worked with him.

THE ACTOR
Willie Sutton's Life of Crime

Willie Sutton was born in Brooklyn in 1901. He left home to find work after the eighth grade. Short-term jobs followed, but none were as lucrative as larceny.

Sutton's adolescence provided an education in crime, as he engaged in various kinds of thievery and possibly even murder. Following a short stint in jail for safecracking in the 1920s, he graduated to bigger robberies, often executed with cunning disguises that gained him the nickname the "Actor." Among them:

- **1930:** New York City bank and a jeweler, dressed as a Western Union messenger
- **1934**: Philadelphia's Corn Exchange Bank and Trust Company, entered through skylight
- **1950:** Queens, New York's Manufacturers Trust Company, netting almost $64,000

Sutton was also an ace escape artist. On February 10, 1947, while serving a life sentence at Pennsylvania's Holmesburg Prison, Sutton and four other convicts scaled the prison walls in a heavy snowstorm while dressed as prison guards. When an actual guard shone a spotlight on them, Sutton yelled, "It's okay" and the escapees made a run for it. The daring breakout garnered so much publicity that the FBI moved Sutton onto its Ten Most Wanted Fugitives list.

THE JFK HIT LIST

Part I

Many mysteries followed the assassination of President John F. Kennedy on November 22, 1963. Conspiracy theorists have frequently pondered the number of people connected to the assassination who died in circumstances some suspected as murder:

- **Hale Boggs:** US senator from Louisiana and member of the Warren Commission. He disappeared on October 16, 1972, in an apparent plane crash in Alaska just days after calling for a new investigation into JFK's death.
- **Rose Cherami**: Told psychiatrists in Louisiana hospital on November 20, 1963, that Kennedy was going to be killed in Dallas. Her skull was crushed by a car on September 4, 1965.
- **David Ferrie:** An unstable pilot linked to Lee Harvey Oswald and the CIA. He was found dead of possible suicide days after being questioned by New Orleans DA Jim Garrison as part of his investigation into the assassination.
- **Dorothy Kilgallen:** Journalist who secured a private interview with Jack Ruby during his spring 1964 trial for killing Lee Harvey Oswald. She was found dead from an apparent suicide on November 8, 1965; she had recently told people she was on her way to New Orleans to "crack the Kennedy case wide open."

THE JFK HIT LIST

Part II

More deaths connected to the assassination of John F. Kennedy, which conspiracy theorists have suggested were targeted killings:

THE BISMARCK TRIBUNE
FINAL
PRESIDENT MURDERED!
New President Johnson, With Him, Isn't Shot
THE DENVER POST
PRESENTS
THE WARREN REPORT
on the Assassination of President Kennedy
THE BISMARCK TRIBUNE
FINAL
Slain President Lies In Death in White House East Room
Confessed Red Charged In Slaying
Second Man Arrested; Dallas Police Note FBI Checked Suspect
World Mourns; Johnson Prays

- **Karyn Kupcinet:** Heard by a long-distance operator screaming into a phone not long before assassination that JFK was going to be killed. Her strangled body was found on November 30, 1963.
- **Grant Stockdale:** Good friend of JFK's with alleged shady connections who died on December 2, 1963, falling from a 13th-floor window in Miami. His death was ruled a suicide though no note was found.
- **Gary Underhill:** Writer with military and CIA connections who said he feared for his life because of what he knew about the conspiracy to kill JFK. He was found dead from a gunshot wound on May 8, 1964; ruled suicide despite inconsistencies in evidence.

Friday, November 20 2026

"**I didn't want to harm the man. I thought he was a very nice gentleman. Soft-spoken. I thought so right up to the moment I cut his throat.**"

—Perry Edward Smith, one of the two men executed for killing the Clutter family in Holcomb, Kansas, in 1959, quoted in Truman Capote's *In Cold Blood*

Saturday, November 21 2026

Sunday, November 22 2026

HAROLD SHIPMAN

Part I: Means and Methods

Dr. Harold Shipman was a general practitioner who started his medical career at a clinic in northern England in 1974. The following year, he was fined and forced into rehab after being caught forging synthetic opioid prescriptions to feed his addiction. But once that was over, Shipman appeared to return to a regular life as an average married-with-four-kids workaday doctor. It wasn't until decades later that he would be nicknamed "Dr. Death."

The most prolific known serial killer in British history, Shipman is believed to have murdered more than 250 people over a period of roughly two decades. Unlike many serial killers, who trawl for victims in deserted places and often come up with complex luring strategies, Shipman's occupation made him more like a spider in a web.

Most of Shipman's victims were in fact the people who trusted him most: his patients.

Monday, November 23 2026

HARDOLD SHIPMAN

Part II: House Calls

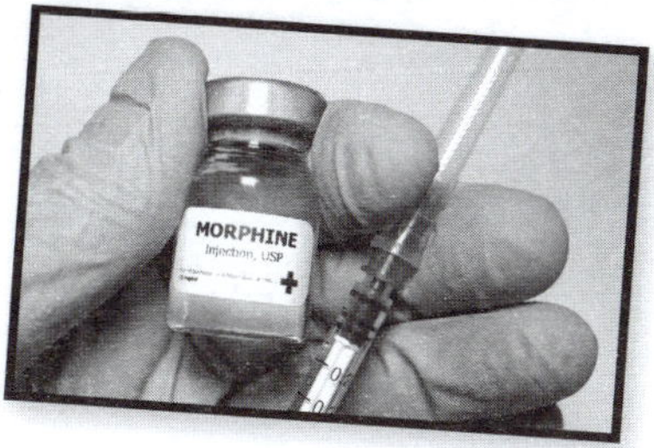

Dr. Harold Shipman was arrested on September 7, 1998. The previous month, police had exhumed the body of one of Shipman's patients, Kathleen Grundy. An examination of her remains found that she was given a lethal dose of morphine. After Shipman's arrest, police discovered a typewriter that appeared to have been used to forge Grundy's will before her death, making him her sole beneficiary.

Post-arrest investigations determined that Shipman followed a pattern with most of his victims:

- Choose a victim, generally though not always an elderly woman.
- Establish a close and trusting relationship (Shipman was known for his bedside manner).
- Administer a lethal dose of morphine during a home visit.
- Steal jewelry (police later found dozens of pieces of stolen jewelry in a box belonging to Shipman's wife).
- Forge death certificate with an invented cause of death (often heart attack or stroke).
- Suggest cremation for elimination of evidence.

HAROLD SHIPMAN

Part III: Dr. Death

Following Dr. Harold Shipman's September 1998 arrest, authorities realized that Kathleen Grundy was likely not the first person he had murdered. Police had actually investigated Shipman earlier that year after another doctor reported her concerns, but he had ultimately been cleared. It was later suggested in an official report that three of Shipman's victims might have been saved if the first investigation had been appropriately thorough.

Shipman went on trial in October 1999. In 2000, he was found guilty of murdering 15 patients and sentenced to life in prison. A larger investigation covering Shipman's entire medical career discovered a litany of horrors:

- His first victim likely was murdered in 1972.
- Between 1977 and 1992, he killed at least 71 people in one clinic.
- Going into practice on his own in 1992, he began killing at a faster rate. By 1997, he may have been claiming a victim every 10 days.
- By the time of the first failed investigation in March 1998, he had taken at least 240 lives.

"Dr. Death" was never tried for most of his crimes. He died by suicide in his prison cell in January 2004, age 57.

"Serial killers prey on the vulnerable . . . those people who do not feel able to answer back to those whom this structure adorns with power—often the power of life and death. . . . Shipman's murders should have been contributing to a debate about the place of the elderly. The fact that this has not happened means it is all the more likely that he will not be this country's last serial killer."

—David Wilson, professor of criminology

CRIME FAILS

Drugs, Drugs, and Money

On May 10, 2024, the sheriff and chief deputy of Kentucky's Clay County were called to investigate a report of a man passed out in his car. They found 43-year-old David Ratliff indeed unconscious at the wheel of his vehicle in a store parking lot in the town of Manchester.

As is common practice, the police woke Ratliff and asked him for his ID. Somewhat unusually, Ratliff instead handed over his stash:

- 9 grams of methamphetamine
- Fentanyl pills
- $3,034 in cash

Unsurprisingly, Ratliff was arrested.

"Expose the crime, and hunt down the criminal; but remember that even in the case of crime, if it is attacked in sensational, lurid, and untruthful fashion, the attack may do more damage to the public mind than the crime itself."

—Theodore Roosevelt, "*The Man with the Muck Rake*" speech, April 15, 1906

Saturday, November 28 2026

Sunday, November 29 2026

TERMINOLOGY

Entomology

This is the scientific study of arthropods (i.e., a range of jointed-leg invertebrates ranging from spiders to crabs and various insects). Forensic entomologists are sometimes called in to study insects who lay eggs in decomposing bodies as a way of determining cause or time of death.

Monday, November 30 2026

KAITLIN ARMSTRONG
On the Run

On May 11, 2022, gunshots were heard coming from an apartment in Austin, Texas, where Anna Moriah Wilson was found bleeding from several fatal gunshot wounds. An up-and-coming star in professional cycling, Wilson had been swimming earlier in the day with Colin Strickland, a cyclist whom she had dated the previous fall.

Six days after Wilson's killing, police issued an arrest warrant for Kaitlin Armstrong, a former girlfriend of Strickland's whose Jeep had been seen near the apartment where the murder happened.

The hunt proved more difficult than expected. Armstrong sold her Jeep and used a fake passport to fly to Costa Rica, where she tried to hide out. She used aliases, changed her appearance with plastic surgery, and tried to start up a yoga business in a tourist-popular village.

US marshals apprehended Armstrong in June 2022 after enticing her by taking out an ad on Facebook for her yoga business. She was found guilty of Wilson's murder in November 2023.

FLORIDA MAN (AND WOMAN) CRIMES

This unscientific roundup of criminal activities have an unmistakable Florida-ness to them:

- **October 2023, Polk County, Florida:** Sheriff's deputies looking to arrest Johnny Yates for aggravated battery were not fooled by the sign he had put up outside the house where he was staying, which read, "Johnny Yates does NOT live here!"
- **May 2022, Key Largo, Florida:** Police attempted to pull over Janiya Shaimiracle Douglas, who refused to stop her vehicle. Once she was taken into custody, Douglas told officers she had had "getting arrested" on her "bucket list" since high school and could now cross it off.
- **June 2017, Merritt Island, Florida:** Jonathan Hinkle was arrested for misusing emergency services after calling 911 in an attempt to get a ride to Hooters (his original ride, his grandmother, couldn't drive him because she had had a stroke).

"**All right, warden. Let's give them what they want.**"

—Melvin White, executed by lethal injection in Huntsville, Texas, on November 3, 2005. White was convicted of kidnapping, raping, and murdering nine-year-old Jennifer Lee Gravell in 1997.

TRUE CRIME QUIZ

True or false?

Lizzie Borden was convicted for the 1892 axe murder of her father and stepmother.

Answer: False. Borden was acquitted because the evidence against her was only circumstantial.

ART FOR THEFT

Part I: Who Wants a Picasso?

According to the Art Loss Register, a private database of lost and stolen art that serves the art and insurance markets, these artists share the uncommon distinction of having the most pieces stolen:

1. Pablo Picasso: 1,147
2. Nick Lawrence: 557
3. Marc Chagall: 516
4. Karel Appel: 505
5. Salvador Dali: 505
6. Joan Miró: 478
7. David Levine: 343
8. Andy Warhol: 343
9. Rembrandt Harmenszoon van Rijn: 337
10. Peter Reinicke: 336

ART FOR THEFT

Part II: Priceless

In 1990, Boston's Isabella Stewart Gardner Museum was broken into by two thieves who stole 13 paintings. It was one of the most sensational art heists of all time. Adding a layer of mystery, the pieces were never recovered despite a massive search. Among the works were several that are so valuable some appraisers consider them literally priceless, including Rembrandt's *Christ in the Storm on the Lake of Galilee*. One painting does have a price tag, though: Vermeer's *The Concert*, appraised at roughly $200 million.

Some of the other most valuable paintings stolen in the 20th century include:

- *Poppy Flowers* by Vincent van Gogh (stolen 2010): $55 million
- *The Scream* by Edvard Munch (stolen 1994 and 2004, later returned): $120 million
- *Frances Bacon* by Lucien Freud (stolen 1988): $35 million
- *Waterloo Bridge, London* by Claude Monet (stolen 2012): $35 million

TERMINOLOGY

Parricide

This terms describes the act when a person kills one or both of their parents; also used to describe the killing of a close relative.

"Because that's where the money is."

—Willie Sutton, when asked why he robbed banks

Wednesday, December 9 2026

CRIME STATS

The McMartin preschool case began when the mother of a student at a family-run preschool in Manhattan Beach, California, alleged the child had been abused by one of the teachers. The number of allegations quickly exploded, taking on increasingly hard-to-fathom charges (including accusations of Satanic rituals). The scandal turned into one of the largest such cases in US history. It was later viewed as one of the most egregious examples of the period's so-called "Satanic panic."

- **Duration of trials:** 1987–1990
- **Witnesses called:** 124
- **Exhibits presented:** 800
- **Total cost:** $15 million
- **Convictions:** 0

In the end, the defendants were acquitted, and the investigation was discredited for its use of leading questions and other unreliable methods.

THE END OF ARTURO GATTI

A scrawny kid from Montreal, Canada, Arturo Gatti was one of the most celebrated lightweight boxers of the 1990s. Gatti won 40 of his 49 professional fights, 31 by knockout. Though Gatti was never a household name, his three fights with Micky Ward in the early 2000s achieved legendary status.

Gatti's life outside the ring was often chaotic, given his reputation for partying, getting into fights, and multiple drunk driving arrests. After ending his boxing career in 2007, he married and soon fathered a child with Amanda Rodrigues, a Brazilian immigrant 14 years his junior. The marriage was tumultuous, and Gatti was cited for domestic violence. But when they took a trip to Europe and Brazil in 2009, it seemed that things were on the mend—or were they?

On July 11, 2009, Gatti was found dead at a hotel in Brazil. Rodrigues was arrested for murder because security cameras did not show anyone else entering their room. Later, his death was ruled a suicide by hanging, but friends of Gatti suggested something darker. They claimed that the couple had drawn up a new will before the trip that left his millions to Rodrigues and their son and that she had killed him for the money.

THE KIDNAPPING OF ALDO MORO

Aldo Moro was one of the best-known politicians in Italy. He had been a five-time prime minister and, in 1978, he was getting ready to run for prime minister for a sixth time. But on March 16, four members of the leftist terror group the Red Brigade ambushed Moro's motorcade in Rome as he was on his way to finalize a historic pact between two of the country's major parties. A volley of gunfire killed Moro's bodyguards, and he was taken captive.

Over the next several weeks, the Red Brigade demanded the government release several of their imprisoned comrades in exchange for Moro. The government refused to negotiate, even after Moro wrote several plaintive letters asking for his life to be spared. Despite a massive nationwide manhunt, authorities could not find him.

Moro was shot dead by Red Brigades leader Mario Moretti on May 9.

Likely knowing how his story was going to end and that he would not be saved by those in power, Moro sent a final letter to his wife two days before his death. He told her, "I kiss you for the last time" and asked that no politicians be invited to his funeral.

TERMINOLOGY

Do the Houdini

This is the code name given by the Hell's Kitchen Irish gang, the Westies, in the 1970s and 1980s to their preferred disposal method for victims' bodies: cutting them apart, putting the pieces into garbage bags, and tossing the whole lot into New York City's East River.

"I cannot understand honest men. They lead desperate lives full of boredom."

—Victor Lustig, a con man most famous for selling the Eiffel Tower—twice

DEAD BY HIS OWN GUN

On May 27, 2021, in the Belize island tourist town of San Pedro, Jasmine Hartin and her common-law husband, Andrew Ashcroft, were invited to their friend Henry Jemmott's nearby beachfront apartment. Ashcroft decided to stay at home, so Hartin went alone. There was drinking, and at some point after midnight, Jemmott—the local police superintendent—died from a gunshot wound to the head by his own Glock pistol.

Hartin's story was that she and Jemmott had gone for a walk along the water, he had showed her the pistol, and the gun accidentally went off when she was handing it back.

Authorities were not convinced and arrested Hartin on May 31 for manslaughter by negligence. The story made international news largely because of Hartin's wealth and social connections; she was a luxury real-estate developer from Canada and her husband's father was the conservative British politician-billionaire Lord Michael Ashcroft. The combination of Hartin's high profile and the disputed nature of the crime sparked somewhat salacious rumors. Some suggested that Jemmott had killed himself, and others said that Hartin had been giving Jemmott a massage not long before the shooting. Amid the chaos, Ashcroft left her and took their children out of Belize.

Hartin pleaded guilty to the manslaughter charge in April 2023.

CALL ME HOLDEN
Mark David Chapman

On December 8, 1980, Mark David Chapman left his New York City hotel room to buy a new copy of *The Catcher in the Rye* by J. D. Salinger. This was not a random act. As Chapman told an interviewer decades later, he had been "literally living inside" the book, marinating in the dyspeptic worldview of its misanthropic, immature, Manhattan-wandering protagonist, Holden Caulfield.

Chapman walked up to the Dakota apartment building on Central Park West. He waited outside, reading his copy of *Catcher*, inside of which he had written, "This is my statement" and signed, "Holden Caulfield."

He had also been obsessing over another cultural artifact: the 1970 album *John Lennon/Plastic Ono Band*. Listening to the song, "God," where John Lennon signs, "I don't believe in Bible . . . I don't believe in Jesus . . . I don't believe in Beatles," Chapman became furious about Lennon, wondering, *Who does he think he is?*

Later that night, when Lennon and Yoko Ono were returning home, Chapman killed Lennon with four pistol shots to his back.

Chapman later pleaded guilty to the murder. True to form, at his 1981 sentencing hearing, when asked if he wanted to make a statement, he read a passage from *Catcher*.

TRUE CRIME QUIZ

True or false?

Female serial killers are more likely than males to murder strangers.

Answer: False. A 2019 study of 110 serial killers evenly divided by gender found that males were about six times more likely to kill strangers than females. The male serial killers were also far more likely to stalk their victims first; in the sample studied, only two of the studied female serial killers were stalkers.

"I don't do anything like that and I don't know anyone who would do a thirteen-year-old child."

—Terry Harper, describing what he said to his sister-in-law, Wanda Holloway, in 1991. According to Harper, Holloway had asked if he could hire someone to kill a teenage girl who had beaten out Holloway's daughter for a spot on the high school cheerleading squad and the girl's mother. After two sensational trials, Holloway served six months in prison for the plot.

STÉPHANE BOURGOIN
The Serial Killer Expert Who Wasn't

During the 1970s, Stéphane Bourgoin worked in and around the B-movie industry. He reviewed horror flicks for fanzines, briefly worked on some movie sets in the United States, and wrote some porn films. In the 1990s, Bourgoin started to develop a new career: serial killer expert.

Bourgoin wrote dozens of books about killers, many of whom he said he had interviewed in prison. His books became bestsellers and his fame turned him into something of a celebrity in European true crime circles. He claimed he was even sought out for advice and trained at Quantico by the FBI. He frequently told a dramatic origin story for his obsession: While living in LA in 1976, he discovered his then-girlfriend, "Eileen," murdered by a killer who had raped and mutilated her.

In 2020, online investigators revealed Bourgoin had lied about most aspects of his past. He quickly admitted to being a serial fabulist. Most of his serial killer interviews (such as one with Charles Manson) had never happened. There was no murdered girlfriend. No FBI connection. Bourgoin apologized profusely, though he said to a writer from the *New Yorker*, "But I never raped or killed anybody."

Monday, December 21 2026

"I am deeply hurt by your calling me a woman hater. I am not. But I am a monster."

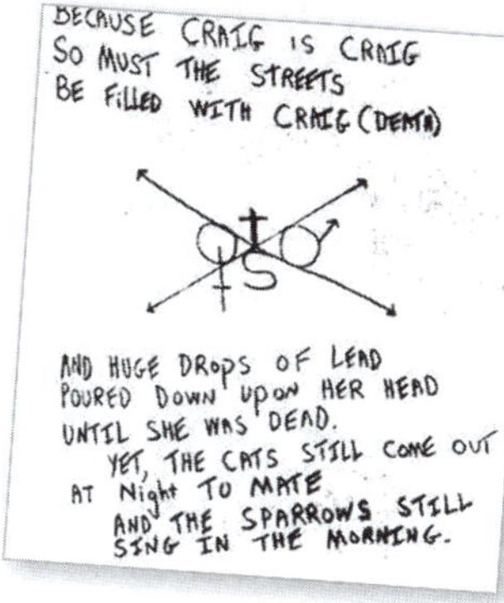
BECAUSE CRAIG IS CRAIG
SO MUST THE STREETS
BE FILLED WITH CRAIG (DEATH)

AND HUGE DROPS OF LEAD
POURED DOWN UPON HER HEAD
UNTIL SHE WAS DEAD.
YET, THE CATS STILL COME OUT
AT NIGHT TO MATE
AND THE SPARROWS STILL
SING IN THE MORNING.

—David "Son of Sam" Berkowitz's first letter to New York City police, received on April 17, 1977

JOHN WAYNE GACY
A Very Picky Murderer

Serial killer John Wayne “The Killer Clown” Gacy was sentenced to death in 1980 for murdering 33 young men and boys. Because of the fame that came from his grotesque record, while waiting at the Menard Correctional Center in Illinois for his execution, Gacy sometimes received mail from people wanting to interview him.

Before agreeing to speak with anyone, Gacy would demand the interviewer fill out a handmade questionnaire that he mailed them. It included these questions:

- Childhood hero
- Hobbies
- If I were president I’d . . .
- Favorite color
- My advice to children

In at least one case, Gacy provided some of his answers. He viewed himself as “a positive thinker, self-starter, open minded, nonjudgmental.” As for favorite song? He was divided between “Amazing Grace” and “Send in the Clowns.”

Wednesday, December 23 2026

ST. PAUL LAYOVER

This unofficial policy was instituted by Police Chief John O'Connor of the St. Paul, Minnesota, Police Department during the early 20th century. His proposition to criminals was simple: Keep your heads down and commit no crimes while you are in town, and the St. Paul police will leave you be. The arrangement was organized enough that new-in-town gangsters were expected to check in with O'Connor's underworld connection William "Reddy" Griffin at the Hotel Savoy downtown.

The layover system worked for a time, with bribes and limited arrests keeping détente and ensuring that St. Paul could serve as a peaceful respite for stressed-out gangsters on the run. But after O'Connor died and a car bomb took out his replacement in 1928, the arrangement fell apart. By the 1930s, crime and corruption were rampant enough in St. Paul that investigations by federal agents and local reformers led to a complete overhaul of the police department.

DARK CHRISTMAS

On Christmas Day 2013, it seemed at first like Melissa Young had a good idea. When Young's neighbor Alan Williamson came to her flat that day, the 37-year-old Edinburgh resident, who had a tattoo of the Virgin Mary on one arm and Lucifer on the other, offered her neighbor a surprise Christmas gift: a pair of sneakers and a 2014 calendar.

Williamson demurred. According to authorities, Young attacked Williamson, keeping him from leaving her flat. She called police, at which point Williamson could be heard in the background saying, "Let me out." She then stabbed Williamson a total of 29 times, killing him.

Young claimed she killed Williamson because the archangel Michael had possessed her body to destroy the demon who had taken hold of Williamson's body. She also said that if he had accepted her Christmas gifts, she never would have stabbed him.

CRIME IS IN THE AIR

Everyone knows there is nothing good about air pollution. It hurts your lungs, makes your eyes itch, and long-term exposure can shorten your lifespan.

But when researchers looked at another aspect of air pollution, they found something else to worry about. The paper "Crime Is in the Air: The Contemporaneous Relationship Between Air Pollution and Crime" found a strong linkage between bad air and bad crimes.

The researchers studied London and found that for every decrease in air quality, there was a significant and predictable rise in crime. Interestingly, it was not just any kind of crime that worsened, but crimes identified as spontaneous rather than premeditated.

All of this provides one more reason to stay inside when possible on those smoggy days.

Saturday, December 26 2026

Kwanzaa begins
Boxing Day

Sunday, December 27 2026

TRUE CRIME QUIZ

Connect these actors to the accused criminal they played.

1. Colin Firth
2. Judd Nelson
3. Joaquin Phoenix
4. Christian Bale

A. Joe Hunt
B. John Dillinger
C. Michael Peterson
D. Billy Flynn

Answer: 1. C. In the 2022 HBO miniseries *The Staircase*, Firth portrayed Peterson, a novelist accused of killing his wife in 2001. **2. A.** The 1987 TV movie *Billionaire Boys Club* starred Nelson as Hunt, the Ponzi scheme operator who was arrested for two murders but later had the charges dropped. **3. D.** Phoenix starred in 1995's *To Die For* as a character based on Flynn, the teenager convicted of helping his adult lover Pamela Smart kill her husband. **4. B.** Bale played Dillinger in Michael Mann's 2009 Prohibition-era gangster film *Public Enemies*.

ROBERT HANSEN

Part I: The Baker

Some lonely and bullied kids turn to books or role-playing games to escape. Robert Hansen, a loner born in a small Iowa town in 1939, turned instead to hunting and, when he was 18, the US Army Reserve. His sense of alienation never seemed to leave him, though. At 21, he was imprisoned for burning down a school bus garage. After a string of other arrests, he moved to Alaska in 1967, where he started his next campaign of revenge.

Like his father, who owned a bakery back in Iowa, Hansen opened a bakery in Anchorage. But while he kept up appearances as a small business owner with a wife and children, Hansen also kept up with his petty and later not-so-petty crimes. Although arrested multiple times in the 1970s (theft, rape, and attempted rape), he served only nominal time behind bars—a fact that came back to haunt authorities later.

At that time, Anchorage was booming from oil pipeline construction. This provided Hansen with a continually refreshing population of dancers and sex workers who he began stalking, kidnapping, and killing around 1973.

ROBERT HANSEN

Part II: The Hunter

Robert Hansen, the seemingly mild-mannered Anchorage, Alaska, small business owner and award-winning hunter, was leading a double life. Unknown to the small group of people who knew him, Hansen was engaged in a malevolent habit of stalking, kidnapping, raping, and often murdering women. He would soon became known as the "Butcher Baker."

Hansen later admitted to killing 17 women and raping another 30 from the 1970s into the early 1980s. He would sometimes tie up his victims and fly them in a small plane to the wilderness, where he would kill them. In a sadistic twist, he would sometimes release the women into the wild first so that he could hunt them down.

Incredibly, in 1983, one of his intended victims escaped: Cindy Paulson, a 17-year-old sex worker who Hansen had abducted at gunpoint, raped, and tortured. He was about to put her into his plane when she got free. But even though Paulson was able to clearly identify him to police, he was not arrested until the FBI became involved and a search of his house found numerous trophies from victims and even a map with numerous markings that matched where victims' bodies had been found.

Given a 461-year sentence, Hansen died in prison in 2014.

CORPORATE HOMICIDE

In a curious twist of law, corporations in the United States are at times legally defined as "persons." This generally keeps shareholders from responsibility for damages the corporations may cause. However, sometimes employees may still be charged with serious crimes based on actions they helped undertake. Here are some examples:

- **2018:** Chiquita Brands International settled with the families of six Americans killed by FARC militants in Colombia; Chiquita had previously admitted to paying protection money to FARC.
- **1985:** Three executives of Film Recovery Systems were found guilty of murder after unsafe working conditions led to the death of a worker by cyanide poisoning.
- **1984:** Six Flags was charged with manslaughter after eight teenagers died in a fire at a New Jersey amusement park.

PHOTO CREDITS

COVER AND TITLE PAGE PHOTO INSETS (clockwise starting from top right): Vince Bucci/AFP/Getty Images, K True-Crime/Pixels, Hilda Weges/Getty Images, RGR Collection/Alamy Stock Photo.

INTERIOR: Alamy: Marcos Alvarado 1/12, CBW 11/19, Everett Collection Historical 3/25, 6/10, Everett Collection Inc 2/12, James Jackson 7/16, Johnny Jones 10/12, Susie Kearley 9/30, Keystone Press 8/13, 8/22–23, Patti McConville 10/20, Trinity Mirror/Mirrorpix 6/20–21, Serge Mouraret 9/15, Michael Neelon (misc) 7/7, NiKreative 4/16, North Wind Picture Archives 11/28–29, PA Images 8/10, Pictorial Press Ltd. 2/6, Portrait Essentials 5/8, RGR Collection 1/2, ruelleruelle 5/12, Welsh Designs/Stockimo 11/6, Xinhua 1/8, YAY Media AS 6/9, ZUMA Press, Inc. 1/29. **AP Images:** AP Photo 6/6–7, FBI/Erie Times-News via AP 1/20, David Handschuh 5/1, Joel Page 1/26, Roberto Pfeil 4/7, Steve Pfost/Newsday via AP 1/30. **Bridgeman:** Look and Learn/Peter Jackson Collection 9/10. **Courtesy Use:** Appalachian Trail Conservancy 3/26, Heritage Pest Control 2/14–15, Lansdowne Family Dental 9/4, The Canadian Press/Mark Blinch 7/9, The Historic Lizzie Borden House 11/17, True Crime Collective 12/23. **Depositphotos:** Rawpixel 7/25–26. **Getty Images:** Antagain 6/8, Bettmann 12/22, Katarzyna Bialasiewicz 9/22, boerescul 4/1, Vince Bucci 5/4, Edoardo Fornaciari 5/30–31, Brian Galbraith 2/3, Aleksandar Georgiev 1/24–25, Getty Images/Stringer 7/31, Nathan Griffith 7/18–19, guvendemir 9/23, Hailshadow 11/24, Janny2 11/30, Daniel Leal 12/5–6, Luna Marina 7/30, natasaadzic 10/5, Dana Neely 1/14, New York Daily News Archive 2/21–22, Scott Olson 4/29, Popperfoto 2/9, Alex Raths 2/23, Frederic Reglain 12/21, Screen Archives 10/3–4, shaunl/E+ 5/18, Herb Snitzer 4/11–12, Reg Speller/Fox Photos 3/17, The Ring Magazine 12/11, Underwood Archives 2/24, Hilda Weges 9/9, Westend61 12/25, Susan Wood 12/17. **Library of Congress:** Library of Congress/LC-DIG-ppmsca-28344 3/5. **Pixels:** Granger 3/12, K True-Crime 9/2. **Public Domain:** Cecilia Bleasdale 11/7–8, Capagmausuian 11/12, Dewsbury Police Station 4/2, FBI 1/14, 4/22, Manual on Uniform Traffic Control Devices 6/13–14, Murderpedia 2/16, 5/23–24, Newspaper.com 11/20. **Shutterstock:** Duncan Andison 2/17, BLGKV 8/7, Dabarti CGI 5/16–17, Nicola Devecchi 12/1, Kelvin Kho 2/26, Christophe Petit Tesson/EPA 11/10, Mark-Wu 11/13, Stephen Mulcahey 8/5, n_defender 6/5, NeagoneFo 6/1, Rix Pix Photography 8/18, solarseven 3/9, TaurusY 5/9–10, Olga Visavi 9/26–27, Westend61 8/27.

2027

JANUARY

S	M	T	W	T	F	S
					1	2
3	4	5	6	7	8	9
10	11	12	13	14	15	16
17	18	19	20	21	22	23
24/31	25	26	27	28	29	30

FEBRUARY

S	M	T	W	T	F	S
	1	2	3	4	5	6
7	8	9	10	11	12	13
14	15	16	17	18	19	20
21	22	23	24	25	26	27
28						

MARCH

S	M	T	W	T	F	S
	1	2	3	4	5	6
7	8	9	10	11	12	13
14	15	16	17	18	19	20
21	22	23	24	25	26	27
28	29	30	31			

APRIL

S	M	T	W	T	F	S
				1	2	3
4	5	6	7	8	9	10
11	12	13	14	15	16	17
18	19	20	21	22	23	24
25	26	27	28	29	30	

MAY

S	M	T	W	T	F	S
						1
2	3	4	5	6	7	8
9	10	11	12	13	14	15
16	17	18	19	20	21	22
23/30	24/31	25	26	27	28	29

JUNE

S	M	T	W	T	F	S
		1	2	3	4	5
6	7	8	9	10	11	12
13	14	15	16	17	18	19
20	21	22	23	24	25	26
27	28	29	30			

JULY

S	M	T	W	T	F	S
				1	2	3
4	5	6	7	8	9	10
11	12	13	14	15	16	17
18	19	20	21	22	23	24
25	26	27	28	29	30	31

AUGUST

S	M	T	W	T	F	S
1	2	3	4	5	6	7
8	9	10	11	12	13	14
15	16	17	18	19	20	21
22	23	24	25	26	27	28
29	30	31				

SEPTEMBER

S	M	T	W	T	F	S
			1	2	3	4
5	6	7	8	9	10	11
12	13	14	15	16	17	18
19	20	21	22	23	24	25
26	27	28	29	30		

OCTOBER

S	M	T	W	T	F	S
					1	2
3	4	5	6	7	8	9
10	11	12	13	14	15	16
17	18	19	20	21	22	23
24/31	25	26	27	28	29	30

NOVEMBER

S	M	T	W	T	F	S
	1	2	3	4	5	6
7	8	9	10	11	12	13
14	15	16	17	18	19	20
21	22	23	24	25	26	27
28	29	30				

DECEMBER

S	M	T	W	T	F	S
			1	2	3	4
5	6	7	8	9	10	11
12	13	14	15	16	17	18
19	20	21	22	23	24	25
26	27	28	29	30	31	

Workman Calendars is an imprint of Workman Publishing, a division of Hachette Book Group, Inc. The Workman name and logo are registered trademarks of Hachette Book Group, Inc. PAGE-A-DAY and the PAGE-A-DAY design/logo are registered trademarks of Hachette Book Group, Inc.

The publisher is not responsible for websites (or their content) that are not owned by the publisher.

Design by Barbie Altorfer
Photo research by Sophia Reith

Cover and title page photos, clockwise from top: Vince Bucci/AFP/Getty Images, K True-Crime/Pixels, Hilda Weges/Getty Images, RGR Collection/Alamy Stock Photo

Workman Calendars may be purchased in bulk for business, educational, or promotional use. For information, please contact your local bookseller or the Hachette Book Group Special Markets Department at special.markets@hbgusa.com.

ISBN 978-1-5235-3189-9

Printed in Thailand

Workman Calendars
Workman Publishing
Hachette Book Group, Inc.
1290 Avenue of the Americas
New York, NY 10104

pageaday.com

workman
CALENDARS

2026

JANUARY

S	M	T	W	T	F	S
				1	2	3
4	5	6	7	8	9	10
11	12	13	14	15	16	17
18	19	20	21	22	23	24
25	26	27	28	29	30	31

FEBRUARY

S	M	T	W	T	F	S
1	2	3	4	5	6	7
8	9	10	11	12	13	14
15	16	17	18	19	20	21
22	23	24	25	26	27	28

MARCH

S	M	T	W	T	F	S
1	2	3	4	5	6	7
8	9	10	11	12	13	14
15	16	17	18	19	20	21
22	23	24	25	26	27	28
29	30	31				

APRIL

S	M	T	W	T	F	S
			1	2	3	4
5	6	7	8	9	10	11
12	13	14	15	16	17	18
19	20	21	22	23	24	25
26	27	28	29	30		

MAY

S	M	T	W	T	F	S
					1	2
3	4	5	6	7	8	9
10	11	12	13	14	15	16
17	18	19	20	21	22	23
24/31	25	26	27	28	29	30

JUNE

S	M	T	W	T	F	S
	1	2	3	4	5	6
7	8	9	10	11	12	13
14	15	16	17	18	19	20
21	22	23	24	25	26	27
28	29	30				

JULY

S	M	T	W	T	F	S
			1	2	3	4
5	6	7	8	9	10	11
12	13	14	15	16	17	18
19	20	21	22	23	24	25
26	27	28	29	30	31	

AUGUST

S	M	T	W	T	F	S
						1
2	3	4	5	6	7	8
9	10	11	12	13	14	15
16	17	18	19	20	21	22
23/30	24/31	25	26	27	28	29

SEPTEMBER

S	M	T	W	T	F	S
		1	2	3	4	5
6	7	8	9	10	11	12
13	14	15	16	17	18	19
20	21	22	23	24	25	26
27	28	29	30			

OCTOBER

S	M	T	W	T	F	S
				1	2	3
4	5	6	7	8	9	10
11	12	13	14	15	16	17
18	19	20	21	22	23	24
25	26	27	28	29	30	31

NOVEMBER

S	M	T	W	T	F	S
1	2	3	4	5	6	7
8	9	10	11	12	13	14
15	16	17	18	19	20	21
22	23	24	25	26	27	28
29	30					

DECEMBER

S	M	T	W	T	F	S
		1	2	3	4	5
6	7	8	9	10	11	12
13	14	15	16	17	18	19
20	21	22	23	24	25	26
27	28	29	30	31		